KMN

Explorations in World Literature

[èksplɔréʃ]
① 쉼서 당사, 탐험.

[lít(ə)ritʃər]
① 문예, 문학 작품

Readings to Enhance Academic Skills

[inhǽns] ① (정도)를 올리다, 늘리다, 호화하고
hanced.:
hancing:

Explorations in World Literature

Readings to Enhance Academic Skills

Carole M. Shaffer-Koros
Kean College of New Jersey

Jessie M. Reppy
Kean College of New Jersey

St. Martin's Press
New York

Editor: Naomi Silverman
Managing editor: Patricia Mansfield-Phelan
Project editor: Talvi Laev/Amy Horowitz
Production supervisor: Alan Fischer
Art director: Sheree Goodman
Text design: Howard Petlack, A. D., A Good Thing Inc.
Photo research: Elsa Peterson
Line Art: Silvia Koros
Maps: Maryland CartoGraphics
Cover design and art: Hothouse Designs, Inc.

8 7 6 5 4
f   e   d   c   b   a

For information, write:
St. Martin's Press, Inc.
175 Fifth Avenue
New York, NY 10010

ISBN: 0-312-08119-7

Acknowledgments

Wolkstein, Diane and Samuel Noah Kramer. "The Huluppu-Tree" from *Inanna, Queen of Heaven and Earth: Her Stories and Hymns from Sumer* by Diane Wolkstein and Samuel Noah Kramer, published by Harper Perennial 1983.

Erodes, Richard and Alfonso Ortiz, ed. "The Well-Baked Man." From *American Indian Myths and Legends* by Richard Erodes and Alfonso Ortiz. Copyright © 1984 by Richard Erodes and Alfonso Ortiz. Reprinted by permission of Pantheon Books, a division of Random House, Inc.

Cook, Albert. Excerpt from *The Odyssey*. Reprinted from *The Odyssey*, Homer, A Norton Critical Edition, translated by Albert Cook, by permission of W. W. Norton & Company, Inc. Copyright © 1974, 1967 by Albert Cook.

Fitts, Dudley and Robert Fitzgerald. Excerpts from *The Antigone of Sophocles: An English Version* by Dudley Fitts and Robert Fitzgerald, copyright 1939 by Harcourt Brace Jovanovich, Inc. and renewed 1967 by Dudley Fitts and Robert Fitzgerald, reprinted by permission of the publisher. Caution: All rights including professional, amateur, motion picture, recitation, lecturing, performance, public reading, radio broadcasting, and television are strictly reserved. Inquiries on all should be addressed to Harcourt Brace Jovanovich, Inc. Permissions Department, Orlando, Florida 32887.

Acknowledgments and copyrights are continued at the back of the book on page 215, which constitutes an extension of the copyright page.

Preface

Explorations in World Literature is an introductory world literature text for all students, whether they are advanced speakers of English as a second language or foreign language, or native speakers of English. This anthology presents complete and excerpted authentic literary selections and is intended to stimulate student interest in multiculturalism. The selections are from diverse cultures and periods of history and provide a balanced racial, ethnic, and gender perspective. Authors from both the traditional English canon and the "new canon" are included.

While learning about literature and world cultures, students will have the opportunity to improve their critical-thinking skills in all four language areas: reading, writing, speaking, and listening. *Explorations in World Literature* is a flexible introductory literature text and is intended to be used with supplementary grammar and/or writing text(s).

The book is informed by several teaching approaches, including (1) **reader-response theory,** which encourages the student to be an active reader and helps him/her to recognize the ambiguity of literary texts, and (2) **content-based language instruction,** which teaches language through academic subject matter. Thus, students using the book improve their English language skills through the study of world literature.

Flexibility

Explorations in World Literature is designed for flexible use in the classroom. The readings are arranged chronologically, from ancient to modern times, in the book and in the table of contents, and may be taught in this order. However, the instructor may choose to group them by themes as suggested in Table 1 (on p. xviii), by genre as shown in Table 2 (on p. xix), or by geographical area as listed in Table 3 (on p. xx). In addition, instructors may choose the number and variety of reading selections and activities they wish to cover with a particular class.

Contents

The book contains 32 literary selections in 26 chapters. Selections include both traditional works of Western literature such as those of Sophocles, Shakespeare, and Chekhov, and culturally diverse pieces by authors such as Naguib Mahfouz, Claribel Alegría, and Paule Marshall, representing many parts of the world and including complete or excerpted works from most major literary forms.

Each selection is representative of the literary tradition of its native culture. To expand students' understanding of the work, each selection is set in an appropriate historico-cultural context.

Explorations in World Literature includes the following features:

- **Peer work in collaborative study groups** is emphasized throughout the text. Study groups can be used to discuss pre-reading questions, to compare notes after mini-lectures, and to work on activities at the end of each chapter. The peer interaction maximizes student learning.

- **World and regional maps** help to orient students geographically; locating works on a **time line** helps them to understand chronological relationships.

- **Pre-reading questions** determine students' prior knowledge about the selection and its content. These questions focus students' attention on the selection. There are no "correct" answers, and not all students will be able to discuss every question.

- The **key terms** listed are important for understanding the cultural background and the literary selections. They are used in the mini-lectures and class discussions.

- The **mini-lectures** provided in the Instructor's Manual further expand the historico-cultural background given in each chapter and introduce the students to the selection. While the instructor is giving the mini-lecture, students have the opportunity to practice their note-taking skills. Additional historico-cultural information is also included in the Instructor's Manual.

- A **list of selected vocabulary** from the reading is included in each chapter. This list is meant to be an aid to the student and is not exhaustive. The entry for a given word indicates how that word functions in its context (what part of speech it is) and provides a brief definition, again based on the context. The first occurrence of a listed vocabulary word is boldfaced in the text. Furthermore, where a new literary genre is introduced, a brief explanation of it is provided at the beginning of the chapter. Additionally, at the end of the book there is a **literary glossary** for student reference.

- **Activities** at the end of each chapter include reading, writing, and sometimes speaking and listening tasks. Instructors have the flexibility to choose appropriate activities for their classes. The activities are followed by suggested additional readings.

- While it is not necessary to do every activity in a chapter, **reading journal assignments** are recommended to help the students to interact with the reading selection. Sample reading journal entries are provided in the manual.

- Periodic **quizzes** in the form of short essay questions are recommended. A sample quiz is included in the manual.

Acknowledgments

We wish to extend special thanks to Kean College faculty who have piloted chapters of *Explorations in World Literature*. These colleagues include Sylvia Mulling, Linnea Tornqvist, and the many adjunct faculty in the English as a Second Language Program. Our thanks also to Barbara Wheeler, director of the Africana Studies Program, for her advice and to Gerald Hillenbrand for his technical assistance. We are especially grateful to the Kean College students from many countries around the world who have used the materials and helped in their development. Moreover, we are indebted to the New Jersey Department of Higher Education for the Humanities grants that helped to initiate this project and to Mark Lender, director of advanced study and research at Kean College, for his assistance in securing the grants.

Also, we would like to thank the following reviewers for providing thoughtful critiques and suggestions: Leslie Freeman, Teachers College, Columbia University; Christine Holten, UCLA; Marianne Phinney, University of Texas at El Paso; Howard Sage, New York University–American Language Institute; Meritt Stark, Henderson State University; Nancy Strickland, New Mexico State University–Dona Ana; and Paul Tucci, University of Maryland at University College and Anne Arundel Community College.

A special thank-you to Stacia and Stanley V. Reppy for the academic foundation they gave their daughter.

We dedicate this book to our husbands: to Robert M. Koros for his unfailing moral and technical support, and to John P. Keker, without whose help and encouragement this book would not have been completed.

Carole M. Shaffer-Koros
Jessie M. Reppy

Contents

Alternate Table of Contents 1: Thematic Groupings   xviii
Alternate Table of Contents 2: Genre Groupings   xix
Alternate Table of Contents 3: Geographical Groupings   xx

Introduction: To the Student   1

1   **"The Huluppu-Tree" from**
     Inanna, Queen of Heaven and Earth
Anonymous (ca. 2000 B.C.E.)
Oral Tradition and Poetry: Epic or Heroic Poem   3
     Background   3
     Pre-Reading Activities   4
     Key Terms   4
"THE HULUPPU-TREE"   **4**
     Vocabulary   8
     Activities   8
     For Further Reading   10

2   **Genesis (Chapters 1 and 2) from the Old Testament**
Anonymous (first century B.C.E.)
Oral Tradition and Poetry: Sacred Text   13
     Background   13
     Pre-Reading Activities   14
     Key Terms   14
GENESIS (CHAPTERS 1 AND 2)   **15**
     Vocabulary   19
     Activities   19
     For Further Reading   20

Additional Reading
"The Well-Baked Man"
Anonymous (recorded in the nineteenth century)
Oral Tradition and Poetry: Sacred Text   20
     Background   20

"THE WELL-BAKED MAN"   **21**

    Activities   22
    For Further Reading   22

3   **From** *The Odyssey*

Homer (eighth century B.C.E.)
Oral Tradition and Poetry: Epic or Heroic Poem   23
    Background   23
    Pre-Reading Activities   23
    Key Terms   24

FROM *THE ODYSSEY*   **24**

    Vocabulary   26
    Activities   27
    For Further Reading   28

4   **From** *Antigone* **from** *The Theban Plays*

Sophocles (496?–406 B.C.E.)
Drama: Tragedy   29
    Background   29
    Pre-Reading Activities   30
    Key Terms   30

FROM *ANTIGONE*   **30**

    Vocabulary   34
    Activities   35
    For Further Reading   36

5   **From "Red Thread Maiden"**

Yuan Chiao (late ninth century)
Fiction: Short Story   39
    Background   39
    Pre-Reading Activities   40
    Key Terms   40

FROM "RED THREAD MAIDEN"   **40**

    Vocabulary   45
    Activities   46
    For Further Reading   47

6   **"Bisclavret" from** *The Lais of Marie de France*

Marie de France (late twelfth century)

Fiction: Short Story   *49*

    Background   49

    Pre-Reading Activities   50

    Key Terms   50

"BISCLAVRET"   **50**

    Vocabulary   55

    Activities   55

    For Further Reading   56

7   **From "The Miller's Tale" from** *The Canterbury Tales*

Geoffrey Chaucer (1340?–1400)

Oral Tradition and Poetry: Verse Narrative   *57*

    Background   57

    Pre-Reading Activities   58

    Key Terms   58

FROM "THE MILLER'S TALE"   **58**

    Vocabulary   65

    Activities   66

    For Further Reading   67

8   **From** *Romeo and Juliet*

William Shakespeare (1564–1616)

Drama: Tragedy   *69*

    Background   69

    Pre-Reading Activities   69

    Key Terms   70

FROM *ROMEO AND JULIET*   **70**

    Vocabulary   76

    Activities   77

    For Further Reading   77

Additional Reading

Sonnet 29

William Shakespeare
Oral Tradition and Poetry: Sonnet   78

    Activities   78

    For Further Reading   78

9   Romantic Poetry

Johann Friedrich von Schiller (1759–1805) and
William Wordsworth (1770–1850)

Oral Tradition and Poetry: Ode and Sonnet   79

    Key Terms   79

    Pre-Reading Activities   79

    Background: Schiller   79

FROM "ODE TO JOY"   **80**

    Vocabulary   81

    Background: Wordsworth   81

"TO TOUSSAINT L'OUVERTURE"   **82**

"MY HEART LEAPS UP WHEN I BEHOLD"   **83**

"THE WORLD IS TOO MUCH WITH US; LATE AND SOON"   **83**

    Vocabulary   84

    Activities   84

    For Further Reading 85

10   "Ain't I a Woman?"

Sojourner Truth (ca. 1797–1883)

Nonfiction: Autobiographial Essay   87

    Background   87

    Pre-Reading Activities   88

    Key Terms   88

"AIN'T I A WOMAN?"   **88**

    Vocabulary   90

    Activities   90

    For Further Reading   90

11   From *Oliver Twist*

Charles Dickens (1812–1870)

Fiction: Novel   93

Background   93
Pre-Reading Activities   94
Key Terms   94

FROM *OLIVER TWIST*   **94**

Vocabulary   97
Activities   98
For Further Reading   98

12   From *The Turn of the Screw* _____

Henry James (1843–1916)
Fiction: Novella   99
Background   99
Pre-Reading Activities   100
Key Terms   100

FROM *THE TURN OF THE SCREW*   **100**

Vocabulary   105
Activities   106
For Further Reading   107

13   From *Uncle Vanya* _____

Anton Chekhov (1860–1904)
Drama: Comedy   109
Background   109
Pre-Reading Activities   110
Key Terms   110

FROM *UNCLE VANYA*   **110**

Vocabulary   114
Activities   116
For Further Reading   116

14   From "Roman Fever" _____

Edith Wharton (1862–1937)
Fiction: Short Story   117
Background   117
Pre-Reading Activities   118
Key Terms   118

FROM "ROMAN FEVER"   **118**

    Vocabulary   123
    Activities   123
    For Further Reading   124

15   From "The Metamorphosis"

Franz Kafka (1883–1924)

Fiction: Short Story   125
    Background   125
    Pre-Reading Activities   126
    Key Terms   126

FROM "THE METAMORPHOSIS"   **126**

    Vocabulary   129
    Activities   130
    For Further Reading   130

16   From *O Pioneers!*

Willa Cather (1873–1947)

Fiction: Novel   131
    Background   131
    Pre-Reading Activities   132
    Key Terms   132

FROM *O PIONEERS!*   **132**

    Vocabulary   135
    Activities   136
    For Further Reading   136

17   From *Rickshaw*

Lao She (1899–1966)

Fiction: Novel   137
    Background   137
    Pre-Reading Activities   138
    Key Terms   138

FROM *RICKSHAW*   **138**

    Vocabulary   140
    Activities   141
    For Further Reading   141

18   From *Things Fall Apart*
Chinua Achebe (b. 1925)
Fiction: Novel   143
      Background   143
      Pre-Reading Activities   144
      Key Terms   145

FROM *THINGS FALL APART*   **145**
      Vocabulary   147
      Activities   148
      For Further Reading   148

19   From *Out of Africa*
Isak Dinesen (1885–1962)
Fiction: Novel   149
      Background   149
      Pre-Reading Activities   150
      Key Terms   150

FROM *OUT OF AFRICA*   **150**
      Vocabulary   153
      Activities   154
      For Further Reading   154

20   From *The Woman in the Dunes*
Kobo Abe (1924–1993)
Fiction: Philosophical Novel   155
      Background   155
      Pre-Reading Activities   156
      Key Terms   156

FROM *THE WOMAN IN THE DUNES*   **156**
      Vocabulary   159
      Activities   159
      For Further Reading   159

21   From *Chronicle of a Death Foretold*
Gabriel García Márquez (b. 1928)
Fiction: Novella   161
      Background   161

Pre-Reading Activities   162
Key Terms   162

FROM *CHRONICLE OF A DEATH FORETOLD*   **163**

Vocabulary   166
Activities   167
For Further Reading   167

22   From "Boys and Girls"

Alice Munro (b. 1931)

Fiction: Short Story   *169*
Background   169
Pre-Reading Activities   169
Key Terms   170

FROM "BOYS AND GIRLS"   **170**

Vocabulary   172
Activities   173
For Further Reading   174

23   From *Fire on the Mountain*

Anita Desai (b. 1937)

Fiction: Novel   *175*
Background   175
Pre-Reading Activities   176
Key Terms   176

FROM *FIRE ON THE MOUNTAIN*   **176**

Vocabulary   179
Activities   181
For Further Reading   181

24   *From The Thief and the Dogs*

Naguib Mahfouz (b. 1911)

Fiction: Novel   *183*
Background   183
Pre-Reading Activities   184
Key Terms   184

FROM *THE THIEF AND THE DOGS*   **184**

Vocabulary   188

Activities   189
For Further Reading   189

25   From *Flowers from the Volcano*

Claribel Alegría (b. 1924)

Oral Tradition and Poetry: Free Verse   191
Background   191
Pre-Reading Activities   192
Key Terms   192

"FLOWERS FROM THE VOLCANO"   **192**

Vocabulary   195
Activities   196
For Further Reading   197

Additional Reading
Sacred Hymn of Sacrifice to Tlaloc
Anonymous (fifteenth century)
Oral Tradition and Poetry: Sacred Text   197
Background   197

SACRED HYMN OF SACRIFICE TO TLALOC   **198**

Activities   199
For Further Reading   199

26   From *Praisesong for the Widow*

Paule Marshall (b. 1929)

Fiction: Novel   201
Background   201
Pre-Reading Activities   202
Key Terms   202

FROM *PRAISESONG FOR THE WIDOW*   **203**

Vocabulary   205
Activities   206
For Further Reading   207

Glossary of Literary Terms   209

Appendix: Genre Descriptions   211

Index   216

About the Authors   218

Alternate Table of Contents 1:
Thematic Groupings

Creation Stories

"The Huluppu-Tree"
Genesis
"The Well-Baked Man"

Coming of Age

Romeo and Juliet
Oliver Twist
Rickshaw
"Boys and Girls"

Human Relations

"The Huluppu-Tree"
The Odyssey
"The Miller's Tale"
Romeo and Juliet
The Turn of the Screw
"Roman Fever"
"The Metamorphosis"

Human Potential

"Ode to Man" from *Antigone*
"Red Thread Maiden"
"Ode to Joy"
Oliver Twist
Uncle Vanya
Rickshaw
Things Fall Apart

Struggle for Personal and
  Political Independence

"Prologue" from *Antigone*
Romeo and Juliet
"To Toussaint L'Ouverture"
"Ain't I a Woman?"
"Flowers from the Volcano"
Praisesong for the Widow

Male-Female Relations

"The Huluppu-Tree"
"Red Thread Maiden"
"Bisclavret"
"The Miller's Tale"
Romeo and Juliet
"Roman Fever"
Chronicle of a Death Foretold
"Boys and Girls"

Relationship between Nature
  and Humans

Sacred Hymn of Sacrifice to Tlaloc
"My Heart Leaps Up When I Behold"
O Pioneers!
Out of Africa
"Flowers from the Volcano"

Philosophical Works

"The World Is Too Much with Us;
  Late and Soon"
"The Metamorphosis"
The Woman in the Dunes
Chronicle of a Death Foretold
Fire on the Mountain
The Thief and the Dogs

Alternate Table of Contents 2: Genre Groupings

Drama	Comedy	*Uncle Vanya*
	Tragedy	*The Theban Plays: Antigone*
		Romeo and Juliet
Fiction	Novel	*Oliver Twist*
		O Pioneers!
		Rickshaw
		Things Fall Apart
		Out of Africa
		Fire on the Mountain
		The Thief and the Dogs
		Praisesong for the Widow
	Philosophical Novel	*The Woman in the Dunes*
	Novella	*The Turn of the Screw*
		Chronicle of a Death Foretold
	Short story	"Red Thread Maiden"
		"Bisclavret"
		"Roman Fever"
		"The Metamorphosis"
		"Boys and Girls"
Nonfiction	Autobiographical Essay	"Ain't I a Woman?"
Oral Traditions and Poetry	Epic or Heroic Poem	*Inanna, Queen of Heaven and Earth*
		The Odyssey
	Free Verse	"Flowers from the Volcano"
	Odes and Sonnets	"Ode to Joy"
		"To Toussaint L'Ouverture"
		"My Heart Leaps Up When I Behold"
		"The World Is Too Much with Us; Late and Soon"
		Sonnet 29
	Sacred Texts	Genesis
		"The Well-Baked Man"
		Sacred Hymn of Sacrifice to Tlaloc
	Verse Narrative	"The Miller's Tale"

Alternate Table of Contents 3: Geographical Groupings

Africa	Nigeria	*Things Fall Apart*
	Egypt	*The Thief and the Dogs*
Americas	N. America	"The Well-Baked Man"
	USA	"Ain't I a Woman?"
	USA	*The Turn of the Screw*
	USA	"Roman Fever"
	USA	*O Pioneers!*
	Colombia	*Chronicle of a Death Foretold*
	Canada	"Boys and Girls"
	Central America	"Flowers from the Volcano"
	Mexico	Sacred Hymn of Sacrifice to Tlaloc
	Afro-Caribbean	*Praisesong for the Widow*
Asia	China	"Red Thread Maiden"
	China	*Rickshaw*
	Japan	*The Woman in the Dunes*
	India	*Fire on the Mountain*
Europe	Greece	*The Odyssey*
	Greece	"Ode to Man" from *Antigone*
	England	"The Miller's Tale"
	France	"Bisclavret"
	England	*Romeo and Juliet*
	England	Sonnet 29
	Germany	"Ode to Joy"
	England	"To Toussaint L'Ouverture"
	England	"My Heart Leaps Up When I Behold"
	England	"The World Is Too Much with Us: Late and Soon"
	England	*Oliver Twist*
	Russia	*Uncle Vanya*
	E. Europe	"The Metamorphosis"
	Denmark	*Out of Africa*
Middle East	Middle East	"The Huluppu-Tree"
	Middle East	Genesis

Introduction:
To the Student

Explorations in World Literature will introduce you to literature from many different cultures and times. It will also help you to understand and use important literary terms and concepts. Selections include examples from various literary forms, or genres, such as poetry, drama, and fiction. These selections represent the contemporary global village and will help you to appreciate its multicultural nature.

As you read the selections, you will be observing and discussing what is revealed about culture and cultural values in the literary pieces. Culture is the way in which groups of people organize their lives. It includes their political system, their language, their gender roles, their leisure time, and their social relations.

For each literary selection, your instructor may have you work in study groups of three or four students. You may discuss the pre-reading questions, check one another's notes after the mini-lecture presented by the instructor, provide input for one another's reader-response journals, and work on various activities in study groups.

While working with *Explorations in World Literature*, you will have opportunities to improve your critical-thinking skills as well as your academic skills in all four language areas: reading, writing, speaking, and listening.

The mini-lecture preceding each reading will help to expand your knowledge and give you added practice in a very important academic skill, note-taking during a lecture. The key terms before each lecture will help you to focus your attention on important ideas and information in the mini-lecture. To check the accuracy of your notes, you may compare them with those of other members of your study group.

You may also keep a journal in which you record your reactions, questions, observations, ideas about connections between selections, and, in some cases, assignments. Your instructor can help you to set up this journal. Also, a time line is included in the text to help you understand the chronological relationships among the literary selections. Maps will help to orient you geographically.

We hope that you will enjoy your *Explorations in World Literature* and will find using the text an enriching experience.

Figure 1 • **Map of ancient Mesopotamia and Israel**

1

"The Huluppu-Tree" from *Inanna, Queen of Heaven and Earth*

Anonymous (ca. 2000 B.C.E.)
Oral Tradition and Poetry: Epic or Heroic Poem

Background

"The Huluppu-Tree" is from the beginning of the anonymous Sumerian epic cycle *Inanna, Queen of Heaven and Earth.* The epic dates to about 2000 B.C.E. (before the common era, a nonreligious system of dating) and concerns an important figure in Sumerian mythology. Sumer was the earliest civilization in Mesopotamia, the area between the Tigris and Euphrates rivers in the Middle East and the site of present-day Iraq. New technology enabled the Sumerians to support large numbers of people in urban areas, and, as a result, many city-states were established, connected by a common religion and language. The network of city-states was politically organized as Sumeria.

The Sumerians invented a system of writing, *cuneiform*, that was first used to keep business accounts. The scribe used a stick, or stylus, to press characters into wet clay. The tablets were then baked to preserve them. This ancient poem, lost for many centuries, is taken from clay tablets excavated from the *tell*, or mound, of the city of Nippur. The tablets were discovered and translated by scholars in the twentieth century.

Pre-Reading Activities

1. With your study group, discuss how you think a culture that has no writing transmits important values to future generations.
2. What do you think the earliest forms of writing might have looked like? What materials might have been used? Why might people want to write?

Key Terms

These terms and concepts are important for understanding the culture that created "The Huluppu-Tree." They will be used in the mini-lecture and in class discussion.

B.C.E. (before the common era)   oral tradition
carpentry   polytheistic
city-states   prehistorical
clay   quest
cuneiform   Sumer/Sumerian
domesticate   technology
epic   Tigris and Euphrates rivers
leather-working   weaving
Mesopotamia   ziggurat
myth/mythology

"The Huluppu-Tree"
Anonymous

In the first days, in the very first days,
In the first nights, in the very first nights,
In the first years, in the very first years,

In the first days when everything needed was brought into being,
In the first days when everything needed was properly **nourished**,   5
When bread was baked in the **shrines** of the land,
And bread was tasted in the homes of the land,
When heaven had moved away from earth,
And earth had separated from heaven,
And the name of man was fixed;   10
When the Sky God, An, had carried off the heavens,

Figure 2 • Cylinder-seal impression of Inanna (right center) surrounded by seven stars *(Walters Art Gallery, Baltimore)*

And the Air God, Enlil, had carried off the earth,
When the Queen of the Great Below, Ereshkigal, was given the
    underworld for her **domain**,

He **set sail**; the Father set sail,   15
Enki, the God of Wisdom, set sail for the underworld.
Small windstones were tossed up against him;
Large hailstones were hurled up against him;
Like onrushing turtles,
They charged the **keel** of Enki's boat.   20
The waters of the sea **devoured** the bow of his boat like wolves;
The waters of the sea struck the **stern** of his boat like lions.
At that time, a tree, a single tree, a *huluppu*-tree
Was planted by the banks of the Euphrates.
The tree was **nurtured** by the waters of the Euphrates.   25
The whirling South Wind arose, pulling at its roots
And ripping at its branches
Until the waters of the Euphrates carried it away.

A woman who walked in fear of the word of the Sky God, An,
Who walked in fear of the word of the Air God, Enlil,   30
Plucked the tree from the river and spoke:

"I shall bring this tree to Uruk.
I shall plant this tree in my holy garden."
Inanna cared for the tree with her hand.
She settled the earth around the tree with her foot.   35
She wondered:
"How long will it be until I have a shining **throne** to sit upon?
How long will it be until I have a shining bed to lie upon?"

The years passed; five years, then ten years.
The tree grew thick,   40
But its bark did not **split**.
Then a **serpent** who could not be charmed
Made its nest in the roots of the *huluppu*-tree.
The *Anzu*-bird set his young in the branches of the tree.
And the dark maid Lileth built her home in the trunk.   45
The young woman who loved to laugh **wept**.
How Inanna wept!
(Yet they would not leave her tree.)

As the birds began to sing at the coming of the dawn,
The Sun God, Utu, left his royal bedchamber.   50
Inanna called to her brother Utu, saying:
"O Utu, in the days when the fates were **decreed**,
When abundance overflowed in the land,
When the Sky God took the heavens and the Air God the earth,
When Ereshkigal was given the Great Below for her domain,   55
The God of Wisdom, Father Enki, set sail for the underworld,
And the underworld rose up and attacked him . . .
At that time, a tree, a single tree, a *huluppu*-tree
Was planted by the banks of the Euphrates.
The South Wind pulled at its roots and ripped at its branches   60
Until the waters of the Euphrates carried it away.
I plucked the tree from the river,
I brought it to my holy garden.
I **tended** the tree, waiting for my shining throne and bed.

Then a serpent who could not be charmed   65
Made its nest in the roots of the tree.
The *Anzu*-bird set his young in the branches of the tree,
And the dark maid Lileth built her home in the trunk.
I wept.
How I wept!   70
(Yet they would not leave my tree.)"

Utu, the **valiant** warrior, Utu,
Would not help his sister, Inanna.

As the birds began to sing at the coming of the second dawn,
Inanna called to her brother Gilgamesh, saying: 75
"O Gilgamesh, in the days when the fates were decreed,
When abundance overflowed in Sumer,
When the Sky God had taken the heavens and the Air God the earth,
When Ereshkigal was given the Great Below for her domain,
The God of Wisdom, Father Enki, set sail for the underworld,   80
And the underworld rose up and attacked him.
At that time, a tree, a single tree, a *huluppu*-tree
Was planted by the banks of the Euphrates.
The South Wind pulled at its roots and ripped at its branches
Until the waters of the Euphrates carried it away.   85
I plucked the tree from the river,
I brought it to my holy garden.
I tended the tree, waiting for my shining throne and bed.

Then a serpent who could not be charmed
Made its nest in the roots of the tree,   90
The *Anzu*-bird set his young in the branches of the tree,
And the dark maid Lileth built her home in the trunk.
I wept.
How I wept!
(Yet they would not leave my tree.)"   95

Gilgamesh the valiant warrior, Gilgamesh,
The hero of Uruk, stood by Inanna.
Gilgamesh **fastened** his armor of fifty **minas** around his chest.
The fifty minas weighed as little to him as fifty feathers.
He lifted his bronze ax, the ax of the road,   100
Weighing seven **talents** and seven minas, to his shoulder.
He entered Inanna's holy garden.

Gilgamesh struck the serpent who could not be charmed.
The *Anzu*-bird flew with his young to the mountains;
And Lileth smashed her home and fled to the wild, uninhabited   105
    places.
Gilgamesh then loosened the roots of the *huluppu*-tree;
And the sons of the city, who accompanied him, cut off the branches.
From the trunk of the tree he carved a throne for his holy sister.
From the trunk of the tree Gilgamesh carved a bed for Inanna.

From the roots of the tree she fashioned a *pukku* for her brother.   110
From the crown of the tree Inanna fashioned a *mikku* for Gilgamesh,
    the hero of Uruk.

Vocabulary

decree *(v.)*   to decide
devour *(v.)*   to eat up hungrily or greedily
domain *(n.)*   territory or land under one government or ruler
fasten *(v.)*   to join, connect
keel *(n.)*   main wooden piece extending along the entire length of the
    bottom of a boat
*mina *(n.)*   varying unit of weight and money used in ancient Greece,
    Egypt, and Sumeria, generally equal to 1/60 talent or one pound
nourish *(v.)*   to feed a plant or animal
nurture *(v.)*   to feed; to nourish
pluck *(v.)*   to pull out
*pukku and **mikku** *(n.)*   untranslated Sumerian words for a boy's toy
    hoop and stick, symbols of the gods' power
serpent *(n.)*   snake
set sail *(v.)*   to begin a voyage
shrine *(n.)*   sacred or holy place
split (split, split) *(v.)*   to break apart
stern *(n.)*   rear end of a boat or ship
*talent *(n.)*   ancient unit of weight equal to about 58 pounds
tend *(v.)*   to take care of
throne *(n.)*   chair on which a ruler sits
*underworld *(n.)*   land of the dead
valiant *(adj.)*   brave; courageous
weep (wept, wept) *(v.)*   to cry

Activities

1. With a partner, read lines 1–10 of the poem "The Huluppu-Tree"
   aloud to each other. What do you notice about the language in these
   lines that indicates they were once part of oral tradition? Can you see
   any similar pattern elsewhere in the poem?
2. Lines 1–28 summarize the beginning of time according to the
   Sumerian myth of creation. What are important events in this creation
   story? List them in your journal. Discuss your ideas with your class.

*Denotes low-frequency word.

Figure 3 • Sumerian cuneiform tablet (ca. 9th–8th century B.C.E.) describing the separation of heaven and earth *(University Museum, University of Pennsylvania, Philadelphia)*

3. What specific characteristics of an epic do you see in the poem "The Huluppu-Tree"? (Notice that an important male Sumerian epic hero, Gilgamesh, is included in the poem.) Make notes in your journal.

4. How does Inanna change from the beginning of the poem to the end?

5. In your study group or alone, make a list in your journal of items that are important to Sumerian culture as shown in the poem "The Huluppu-Tree." For example, what does the poem tell us about Sumerian religion? Compare your list with those of other students.

6. Based on your notes and the discussion, write a summary of important cultural information about the Sumerians. If you cite the exact wording of the text, be sure to use quotation marks (". . .") around what you are quoting and give the line number in parentheses. For example:

The poet tells us about an important early Sumerian food by stating that at the beginning of time, "bread was baked in the shrines of the land / And bread was tasted in the homes of the land"(6–7).

7. Based on your notes and the discussion, write an essay on Sumerian oral tradition.

For Further Reading

Kramer, Samuel Noah. *History Begins at Sumer*. Philadelphia: U of Pennsylvania P, 1981.

———. *The Sumerians: Their History, Culture and Character*. Chicago: U of Chicago P, 1963.

Wolkstein, Diane, and Samuel Noah Kramer. *Inanna, Queen of Heaven and Earth: Her Stories and Hymns from Sumer*. New York: Harper, 1983.

Woolley, C. Leonard. *The Sumerians*. New York: Norton, n.d.

Figure 4 • Map of ancient Near East

2

Genesis (Chapters 1 and 2) from the Old Testament

Anonymous (first century B.C.E.)
Oral Tradition and Poetry: Sacred Text

Background

Genesis is the first book of the Bible and the Old Testament. Based on several oral traditions, the Old Testament was assembled by Hebrew scholars in the first century B.C.E. (before the common era). This sacred text is important for a number of major religions and has had an important cultural and literary impact worldwide.

The Old Testament was originally written in Hebrew on a continuous papyrus scroll. Papyrus, made from beaten reeds, was prepared in large quantities in the city of Byblos on the eastern Mediterranean. The word *Bible* originates from *Byblos*. The Greeks divided the text of the Bible into chapters and verses and named the first book Genesis because of its opening line, "In the beginning. . . ." *Genesis* means "beginning" in Greek.

The following selection, from the English version authorized by King James of England in 1611, has been chosen for the beauty of its language. Since this translation of Genesis was written in the seventeenth century, the language is somewhat different from modern English. English is a living, changing language, and therefore it has varied through time. For example, in this selection, notice the forms *hath* instead of *has* and *creepeth* instead of *creeps*. Also notice that because the language is poetic, some of the word order is inverted.

Two Important Sources of the Old Testament

Source	Date	Information about the Text
J (Yahweh)	950 B.C.E.	The deity is called Yahweh (translated as Lord God). Style is vivid, lively, imaginative, and picturesque. Answers most important human questions: Why do we die? Why does evil exist? Originated in the south in Judah, around King Solomon's time. (Solomon dies ca. 930 B.C.E.)
	597 B.C.E.	Nebuchadnezzar, King of Babylon, conquers Jerusalem and exiles the Hebrews to Babylon.
	586 B.C.E.	Nebuchadnezzar again conquers Jerusalem, burns the Temple, destroys the city, and exiles the Hebrews to Babylon.
P (Priestly)	539 B.C.E.	The deity is called God in English translation. Originated from priests at Jerusalem Temple; took shape during Hebrew exile in Babylon in sixth century B.C.E. Concerned with the law, interest in genealogies and precise dates of events. Persian King Cyrus conquers Babylon and allows exiled Hebrews to return to Jerusalem, where they are free to practice Judaism.

Pre-Reading Activities

1. With your study group, discuss what you know about the Bible, the Old Testament, and the New Testament. In what language do you believe the Old Testament was written?

2. With your study group, discuss what important questions about human life you think might be answered in a sacred text such as the Old Testament. Why was it necessary to write these ideas down?

Key Terms

These terms and concepts are important for understanding the cultural background of the Old Testament. These key terms will be used in the mini-lecture and in class discussion.

Abraham	Jew/Judaism
Babylon/Babylonian	Judah
Bible	King Solomon (960–925 B.C.E.)
Byblos	monotheistic
Canaan/Canaanite	Nebuchadnezzar II (605–562 B.C.E.)
Cyrus the Great (600?–529 B.C.E)	New Testament

Genesis
Hebrew *(h'apiru)*
Israel
J (Yahweh) Source
Jacob
Jerusalem

Old Testament (OT)
P (Priestly) Source
papyrus
patriarch
Torah

Genesis (Chapters 1 and 2)

Anonymous

Chapter 1

In the beginning God created the heaven and the earth.

And the earth was without form, and **void**; and darkness was 2
upon the face of the deep. And the Spirit of God moved upon the
face of the waters.

And God said, Let there be light: and there was light. 3

And God saw the light, that it was good: and God divided the 4
light from the darkness.

And God called the light Day, and the darkness he called Night. 5
And the evening and the morning were the first day.

Figure 5 • Re-creation of King Solomon's Temple in Jerusalem (ca. 10th century B.C.E.)

And God said, Let there be a **firmament** in the midst of the   6
waters, and let it divide the waters from the waters.

And God made the firmament, and divided the waters which   7
were under the firmament from the waters which were above the
firmament: and it was so.

And God called the firmament Heaven. And the evening and   8
the morning were the second day.

And God said, Let the waters under the heaven be gathered   9
together unto one place, and let the dry land appear: and it was so.

And God called the dry land Earth; and the gathering together   10
of the waters called he Seas: and God saw that it was good.

And God said, Let the earth bring forth grass, the herb **yield-**   11
ing seed, and the fruit tree yielding fruit after [its] kind, whose seed
is in itself, upon the earth: and it was so.

And the earth brought forth grass, and herb yielding seed after   12
[its] kind, and the tree yielding fruit, whose seed was in itself, after
[its] kind: and God saw that it was good.

And the evening and the morning were the third day.   13

And God said, Let there be lights in the firmament of the   14
heaven to divide the day from the night; and let them be for signs,
and for seasons, and for days, and for years.

And let them be for lights in the firmament of the heaven to   15
give light upon the earth: and it was so.

And God made two great lights; the greater light to rule the   16
day, and the lesser light to rule the night: he made the stars also.

And God set them in the firmament of the heaven to give light   17
upon the earth.

And to rule over the day and over the night, and to divide the   18
light from the darkness: and God saw that it was good.

And the evening and the morning were the fourth day.   19

And God said, Let the waters bring forth abundantly the mov-   20
ing creature that hath life, and **fowl** that may fly above the earth in
the open firmament of heaven.

And God created great whales, and every living creature that   21
moveth, which the waters brought forth abundantly, after their kind,
and every winged fowl after [its] kind: and God saw that it was good.

And God blessed them, saying, Be fruitful, and multiply, and   22
fill the waters in the seas, and let fowl multiply in the earth.

And the evening and the morning were the fifth day.   23

And God said, Let the earth bring forth the living creature after   24
[its] kind, cattle, and creeping thing, and beast of the earth after [its]
kind: and it was so.

And God made the beast of the earth after [its] kind, and cattle 25
after their kind, and every thing that **creepeth** upon the earth after
[its] kind: and God saw that it was good.

And God said, Let us make man in our image, after our like- 26
ness: and let them have **dominion** over the fish of the sea, and over
the fowl of the air, and over the cattle, and over all the earth, and
over every creeping thing that creepeth upon the earth.

So God created man in his own image, in the image of God he 27
created him; male and female created he them.

And God blessed them, and God said unto them, Be fruitful, 28
and multiply, and **replenish** the earth, and **subdue** it: and have dominion over the fish of the sea, and over the fowl of the air, and over
every living thing that moveth upon the earth.

And God said, Behold, I have given you every herb bearing 29
seed, which is upon the face of all the earth, and every tree, in which
is the fruit of a tree yielding seed; to you it shall be for meat.

And to every beast of the earth, and to every fowl of the air, 30
and to every thing that creepeth upon the earth, wherein there is life,
I have given every green herb for meat: and it was so.

And God saw every thing that he had made, and, behold, it was 31
very good. And the evening and the morning were the sixth day.

Chapter 2

Thus the heavens and the earth were finished, and all the
host of them.

And on the seventh day God ended his work which he had 2
made; and he rested on the seventh day from all his work which he
had made.

And God blessed the seventh day, and **sanctified** it: because 3
that in it he had rested from all his work which God created and
made.

These are the generations of the heavens and of the earth when 4
they were created, in the day that the Lord God made the earth and
the heavens,

And every plant of the field before it was in the earth, and 5
every herb of the field before it grew: for the Lord God had not
caused it to rain upon the earth, and there was not a man to **till** the
ground.

But there went up a **mist** from the earth, and watered the 6
whole face of the ground.

And the Lord God formed man of the dust of the ground, and 7 breathed into his **nostrils** the breath of life; and man became a living soul.

And the Lord God planted a garden eastward in Eden; and there he put the man whom he had formed.   8

And out of the ground made the Lord God to grow every tree that is pleasant to the sight, and good for food; the tree of life also in the midst of the garden, and the tree of knowledge of good and evil.   9

And a river went out of Eden to water the garden; and from there it was parted, and became four heads.   10

The name of the first is Pisan: that is it which compasseth the whole land of Havilah, where there is gold;   11

And the gold of that land is good: there is **bdellium** and the **onyx** stone.   12

And the name of the second river is Gihon: the same that **compasseth** the whole land of Ethiopia.   13

And the name of the third river is Tigris: that is it which goeth toward the east of Assyria. And the fourth river is Euphrates.   14

And the Lord God took the man, and put him into the garden of Eden to dress it and to keep it.   15

And the Lord God commanded the man, saying, Of every tree of the garden thou mayest freely eat: 16

But of the tree of the knowledge of good and evil, thou shalt not eat of it: for in the day that thou eatest thereof thou shalt surely die.   17

And the Lord God said, It is not good that the man should be alone; I will make him a help meet for him.   18

And out of the ground the Lord God formed every beast of the field, and every fowl of the air; and brought them unto Adam to see what he would call them: and whatsoever Adam called every living creature, that was the name thereof.   19

And Adam gave names to all cattle, and to the fowl of the air, and to every beast of the field; but for Adam there was not found a help meet for him.   20

And the Lord God caused a deep sleep to fall upon Adam, and he slept: and he took one of his **ribs**, and closed up the flesh instead thereof;   21

And the rib, which the Lord God had taken from man, made he a woman, and brought her unto the man.   22

And Adam said, This is now bone of my bones, and flesh of my flesh: and she shall be called Woman, because she was taken out of Man.   23

Therefore shall a man leave his father and his mother, and   24
shall **cleave** unto his wife: and they shall be one flesh.

And they were both naked, the man and his wife, and were   25
not ashamed.

Vocabulary

*bdellium *(n.)* myrrhlike substance (myrrh—ingredient used in making
   incense, perfume, and medicines; obtained from bushes in Arabia and
   eastern Africa)
*cleave *(v.)* to be faithful to
compass *(v.)* to go around
creep *(v.)* to move slowly
*dominion *(n.)* power to rule
*firmament *(n.)* sky
fowl *(n.)* bird
mist *(n.)* water particles in the air (similar to fog but less dense)
nostril *(n.)* either of the external openings of the nose
onyx *(n.)* semiprecious black stone
replenish *(v.)* to make full again
rib *(n.)* any of the arched bones enclosing the chest cavity
sanctify *(v.)* to make holy
subdue *(v.)* to conquer
till *(v.)* to prepare land for raising crops
void *(adj.)* empty
yield *(v.)* to produce; to give up

Activities

1. With a partner, read Chapter 1, verses 1 through 13, of Genesis out
    loud to each other. What do you notice about the verses that indicates
    they were once part of oral tradition?
2. What important human questions are answered in these portions of
    the Old Testament?
3. Genesis contains two versions of the Hebrew creation story. In your
    study group, try to identify where the first version ends and the sec-
    ond one begins. Justify your answer.

---

* Denotes low-frequency word.

4. In your journal, make a list of the important events and the order in which they occur in each version of the creation. Compare your list with those of other class members. How do the events in the two versions of the creation differ?

5. Look at the way language is used in the two creation stories. In your journal note differences and similarities in the tone and images used in the two versions. Now refer to the table on p. 14 comparing the sources of the Old Testament. On which source do you think the first version of the creation is based? On which source do you think the second version is based? Justify your answers.

6. Using your journal and notes to develop supporting details, write an essay comparing and contrasting the two versions of the creation story in Genesis.

7. Based on your notes and class discussion, write an essay on oral tradition in Genesis.

For Further Reading

Alter, Robert, and Frank Kermode, eds. *The Literary Guide to the Bible.* Cambridge, MA: Havard UP, 1987.
Friedman, Richard Elliot. *Who Wrote the Bible?* New York: Summit, 1987.
The Holy Bible, Containing the Old and the New Testaments. New York: New York Bible Society, n.d.

Additional Reading

"The Well-Baked Man"

Anonymous (recorded in the nineteenth century)
Oral Tradition and Poetry: Sacred Text

Background

This creation story is drawn from the Pima-Papago Indians in the southwestern United States. The tribe lives in adobe pueblos—that is, villages built mainly from clay. Originating in oral tradition, the story was recorded and translated in the 1880s. Coyote, a trickster, is a traditional Native American story figure, sometimes represented as an animal, sometimes as a human.

"The Well-Baked Man"

Anonymous

The Magician had made the world but felt that something was missing. "What could it be?" he thought. "What could be missing?" Then it came to him that what he wanted on this earth was some beings like himself, not just animals. "How will I make them?" he thought. First he built himself an *horno*, an oven. Then he took some clay and formed it into a shape like himself.

Now Coyote was hanging around the way he usually does, and when Magician, who was Man Maker, was off gathering firewood, Coyote quickly changed the shape of that clay image. Man Maker built a fire inside the *horno*, then put the image in without looking at it closely.

After a while the Magician said, "He must be ready now." He took the image and breathed on it, whereupon it came to life. "Why don't you stand up?" said Man Maker. "What's wrong with you?" The creature barked and wagged its tail. "Ah, oh my, Coyote has tricked me," he said. "Coyote changed my being into an animal like himself."

Coyote said, "Well, what's wrong with it? Why can't I have a pretty creature that pleases me?"

"Oh my, well, all right, but don't interfere again." That's why we have the dog; it was Coyote's doing.

So Man Maker tried again. "They should be companions to each other," he thought. "I shouldn't make just one." He shaped some humans who were rather like himself and identical with each other in every part.

"What's wrong here?" Man Maker was thinking. Then he saw. "Oh my, that won't do. How can they increase?" So he pulled a little between the legs of one image, saying, "Ah, that's much better." With his fingernail he made a crack in the other image. He put some pleasant feeling in there somewhere. "Ah, now it's good. Now they'll be able to do all the necessary things." He put them in the *horno* to bake.

"They're done now," Coyote told him. So Man Maker took them out and made them come to life.

"Oh my, what's wrong?" he said. "They're underdone; they're not brown enough. They don't belong here—they belong across the water someplace." He scowled at Coyote. "Why did you tell me they were done? I can't use them here."

So the Magician tried again, making a pair like the last one and placing them in the oven. After a while he said, "I think they're   40 ready now."

"No, they aren't done yet," said Coyote. "You don't want them to come out too light again; leave them in a little longer."

"Well, all right," replied Man Maker. They waited, and then he took them out. "Oh my. What's wrong? These are overdone.   45 They're burned too dark." He put them aside. "Maybe I can use them some other place across the water. They don't belong here."

For the fourth time Man Maker placed his images inside the oven. "Now don't interfere," he said to Coyote, "you give me bad advice. Leave me alone."   50

This time the Magician did not listen to Coyote but took them out when he himself thought they were done. He made them come to life, and the two beings walked around, talked, laughed, and behaved in a seemly fashion. They were neither underdone nor overdone.   55

"These are exactly right," said Man Maker. "These really belong here; these I will use. They are beautiful." So that's why we have the Pueblo Indians.

Activities

1. What are the important events in this story? What does the story explain?
2. You have now read several creation stories. Using your imagination, write your own creation story, including the making of the first human beings.
3. Write an essay comparing and contrasting the creation of human beings in "The Well-Baked Man" with the version in Chapter 2 of Genesis.

For Further Reading

Erdoes, Richard, and Alfonso Ortiz, eds. *American Indian Myths and Legends.* New York: Pantheon, 1984.

Mails, Thomas E. *Plains Indians: Dog Soldiers, Bear Men, and Buffalo Women.* New York: Prentice-Hall, 1985.

Radin, Paul. *The Trickster: A Study in American Indian Mythology.* New York: Schocken, 1972.

CHAPTER **3**

From *The Odyssey*

Homer (eighth century B.C.E.)
Oral Tradition and Poetry: Epic or Heroic Poem

Background

Who was the Greek poet Homer? Was the author one poet or many? Was the poet perhaps not a man but a woman? The answers to these questions about Homer's identity have long been debated by scholars. The most commonly accepted view at present is that Homer was a blind poet who lived between 700 and 850 B.C.E. and came from a Greek colony on the eastern Mediterranean Sea.

Homer's two epics, *The Iliad* and *The Odyssey*, are based on heroic events from Bronze Age Greece (about 1200 B.C.E.). *The Odyssey* consists of 24 books. In the beginning of Book I the poet summarizes the 20-year-long struggle of the hero Odysseus to return home to the island of Ithaca after the Greeks have defeated Troy. The selection also draws a parallel with the return of another Greek hero, Agamemnon, to his home, where a tragic end awaits him. The story of Agamemnon tells Odysseus what he must avoid doing in order to reach home safely.

Pre-Reading Activities

1. With your study group, review what you know about the epic as a literary form.
2. Discuss with your group what you know about the religion of the ancient Greeks. Who were some of the important gods? What were they like?
3. Look at a map of the Mediterranean region, especially Greece and the

surrounding area. How would geography affect the daily life of the ancient
Greeks?

Key Terms

Agamemnon, son of Atreus
Aigisthos, lover of Clytemnestra
archaeological investigations
Bronze Age Greece
Clytemnestra, wife of Agamemnon
epic hero
epithet
invocation
Ithaca

Menelaos, brother of Agamemnon
Mount Olympus
muse
Mycenae
Odysseus/odyssey
Orestes, son of Agamemnon and
    Clytemnestra
Penelope, wife of Odysseus
Troy/Trojan War

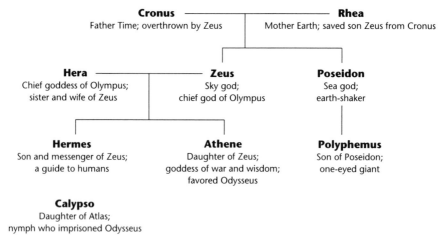

Figure 6 • Gods, goddesses, and supernatural beings in *The Odyssey*

From *The Odyssey*
Homer

Tell me, **Muse**, about the man of many turns, who many
Ways wandered when he had **sacked** Troy's holy **citadel**;
He saw the cities of many men, and he knew their thought;
On the ocean he suffered many pains within his heart,
Striving for his life and his companions' return.   5

But he did not save his companions, though he wanted to:
They lost their lives because of their **recklessness**.
The fools, they devoured the cattle of Hyperion,
The Sun, and he took away the day of their return.
Begin the tale somewhere for us also, goddess, daughter of Zeus.   10
Then all the others, as many as escaped **sheer** destruction,
Were at home, having fled both the war and the sea.
Yet he alone, longing for his wife and for a return,
Was held back in a **hollowed** cave by the queenly **nymph** Calypso,
The divine goddess, who was eager for him to be her husband.   15
But when in the circling seasons the year came around,
The gods **spun** the thread for him to return to his home,
To Ithaca; and he did not escape struggle there either,
Even among his dear ones. All the gods **pitied** him,
Except Poseidon, who **contended unremittingly**   20
With godlike Odysseus, till the man reached his own land.
But the god had gone to the far-off Ethiopians—
The Ethiopians, **remotest** of men, divided **asunder**,
Some where Hyperion sets, and some where he rises.
He was taking part in the sacrifice of bulls and rams,   25
And enjoyed being present at a feast there. The others
Were gathered together in the halls of Olympian Zeus.
The father of men and gods began to speak among them.
In his heart he was remembering excellent Aigisthos
Whom Agamemnon's son, far-famed Orestes, had **slain**.   30
Thinking of that man, he made his speech to the immortals:
"Well now, how indeed mortal men do blame the gods!
They say it is from us evils come, yet they themselves
By their own recklessness have pains beyond their **lot**.
So this Aigisthos married beyond his lot the lawful   35
Wife of the son of Atreus, and killed him on his return;
Knowing he would be destroyed, since we told him beforehand:
We had sent sharp-eyed Hermes, the slayer of Argos,
To tell him not to kill the man and not to **woo** his wife,
Or payment would come through Orestes, descendant of Atreus,   40
As soon as he came of age and **longed for** his own land.
So Hermes told him; but, though of good mind himself, he did not
Change Aigisthos's mind. And now he has paid for it all."
Then the bright-eyed goddess Athene answered:
"Our father, son of Cronus, highest of all rulers,   45
As for that man, he surely lies in a fitting death.
May anyone else also **perish** who would do such deeds.

But the heart within me is torn over skillful Odysseus,
The hard-fated man, who long suffers griefs far from his **dear** ones
On a flood-circled island where the **navel** of the sea is.   50
The island is wooded, a goddess there has her dwelling,
The daughter of destruction-minded Atlas, who knows
The depths of the whole sea, and holds apart earth and heaven.
His daughter has kept back the **wretched** and grieving man,
And perpetually, with tender and **wheedling** speeches,   55
She charms him to forget Ithaca. Odysseus, however,
Wanting to catch sight even of smoke leaping up
From his own land, is longing to die. But your own heart
Does not turn toward it, Olympian one. Did Odysseus
Not please you in broad Troy by the ships of the [Greeks]   60
When he made sacrifice? Why, then, are you so angry at him, Zeus?"
In answer to her, cloud-gathering Zeus spoke out:
"My child, what sort of word has gotten past the bar of your teeth?
How could I at any time forget godlike Odysseus,
Who stands out among mortals for thought, and for the sacrifices   65
He has given the immortal gods who possess broad heaven?
But Poseidon, who holds up the earth, remains **obstinately**
Enraged about the Cyclops whom he blinded in the eye,
Godlike Polyphemus, [his son of great] strength. . . .
For that, to be sure, earth-shaking Poseidon has not   70
Killed Odysseus but makes him wander far from his homeland.
Well, come now, let all of us here carefully **devise**
His return, so he may arrive; and Poseidon will **slacken**
His rage, for **counter** to all the immortals he cannot
Carry on the **strife** alone against the will of the gods."   75

Vocabulary

*asunder *(adv.)*   into parts; apart
citadel *(n.)*   fortress
contend *(v.)*   to struggle
counter *(adv.)*   opposite
dear *(adj.)*   loved
devise *(v.)*   to plan to bring about
enraged *(adj.)*   filled with rage or extreme anger
hollowed *(adj.)*   concave; sunken
long for *(v.)*   to feel a strong desire for
lot *(n.)*   share

* Denotes low-frequency word.

*Muse *(n.)*   any of the nine sister goddesses in Greek mythology
     presiding over the arts and sciences, especially song and poetry
*navel *(n.)*   central point; middle
*nymph *(n.)*   any of the minor divinities of nature in classical
     mythology, represented as beautiful maidens living in mountains,
     forests, trees, and waters
obstinately *(adv.)*   stubbornly
perish *(v.)*   to die
pity *(v.)*   to feel sympathetic sorrow for
recklessness *(n.)*   disregard for the possible consequences (of an action)
remote *(adj.)*   distant
sack *(v.)*   to strip of valuables; to loot, especially a defeated city
sheer *(adj.)*   total; absolute
slacken *(v.)*   to lessen
slay (slew, slain) *(v.)*   to kill
spin (spun, spun) *(v.)*   to draw out and twist fiber into yarn or thread
strife *(n.)*   fight; struggle
strive (strove, striven) *(v.)*   to struggle for
*unremittingly *(adv.)*   constantly
*wheedle *(v.)*   to influence by soft words
woo *(v.)*   to court a woman
wretched *(adj.)*   distressed in body or mind

Activities

1. Because he is an epic hero, Odysseus must have qualities that were
    admired by the ancient Greeks. For example, what epithet does Homer
    use to describe Odysseus? With your study group, read the poem
    closely and make a list in your journal of these good qualities.
    Compare your list with the lists made by the rest of the class.

2. Why is Poseidon, the god of the sea, angry at Odysseus? How does he
    show his anger? Why would Poseidon be important to the Greeks?

3. In his epic poem, Homer shows the importance of narration by telling
    a story within a story. For example, within the main story about
    Odysseus, the god Zeus tells us the story of Aigisthos. In your study
    group, look at the details of the story about Aigisthos and those of the
    story about Odysseus. How are they similiar? How are they different?
    What moral lesson do you think the story of Aigisthos teaches?

4. In your study group, look at the details of the poem again. Make a list
    in your journal of ideas you believe were important to the Greeks of
    Homer's time. Compare your list with the lists made by the rest of the
    class.

5. An epic poem combines realistic details with the fantastic. Look again
    at the text, and make notes in your journal about which events in the

poem seem to be realistic and which are fantastic (not real). Discuss your findings with the class.

6. Using your notes and details from discussion, write a summary of the events Homer describes in this portion of Book I of *The Odyssey*.

7. Using your notes and your journal, write an essay on Odysseus as an epic hero.

8. Write an essay comparing the Greek gods with the Sumerian gods or with God in Genesis.

For Further Reading

Bowra, C. M. *Heroic Poetry*. London: Macmillan, 1964.

Burkert, Walter. *Structure and History in Greek Mythology and Ritual*. Berkeley: U of California P, 1979.

Dimock, George E. *The Unity of The Odyssey*. Boston: U of Massachusetts P, 1989.

Murray, Gilbert. *The Rise of the Greek Epic*. London: Oxford UP, 1967.

Parry, Adam, ed. *The Making of Homeric Verse: The Collected Papers of Milman Parry*. London: Oxford UP, 1971.

4

From *Antigone*
from *The Theban Plays*

Sophocles (496?–406 B.C.E.)
Drama: Tragedy

Background

Tragedy is one of the most important contributions of the ancient Greeks to civilization. The origins of the Greek tragedy have been traced back to the prehistorical worship of Dionysus, a Greek god associated with wine and spring fertility. Female worshippers of the god drank wine and, in a drunken state, sang and danced to honor him.

By the end of the sixth century B.C.E., worship of Dionysus had become civilized. The god was honored in large open-air theaters at annual spring competitions in which prizes were given to the best plays. The religious significance of the performances meant that business was suspended, and every Greek, regardless of class or gender, was expected to attend.

Antigone is a Greek tragedy written by Sophocles. A major competitor and winner in the dramatic contests of the fifth century B.C.E., Sophocles was one of the three most famous tragedians of his time. Based on myths known to the ancient Greek audience, the play concerns the struggle of the young Antigone to bury her brother against the wishes of her uncle, Creon, king of Thebes. Creon makes the gods angry by refusing to allow the burial, and therefore he must be punished for his religious sin.

The Prologue is the opening scene of the tragedy, in which the sisters, Antigone and Ismene, introduce the conflict. The second passage, "Ode to Man," is sung by the Greek chorus and explores the potential and the limits of human beings.

Pre-Reading Activities

1. With your study group, discuss why a culture would want to drama-
   tize certain events in its history. What kinds of events would they
   probably act out?
2. Using a good reference work, research the differences between
   mythology and religion. You should also consider what you have
   learned so far in your reading. You may also view "The Power of
   Myth," a videotaped interview with Joseph Campbell. Discuss your
   ideas with your group.

Key Terms

Learn these important terms and concepts to better understand
the importance of drama and tragedy to the ancient Greek and modern
Western cultures. They will be used in the mini-lecture and in discussion.

Aeschylus (525–456 B.C.E.)	ode
Antigone	Oedipus, former king of Thebes
Aristotle (384–322 B.C.E.)	orchestra
chorus	Pericles/Periclean Athens
conflict	Polyneices
Creon, king of Thebes	protagonist
Dionysus/Dionysia	scene
Eteocles	Thespis/thespian
Euripides (480?–406 B.C.E.)	tragedy
Iocaste	tragic flaw
Ismene	tragic hero
Legend of Thebes	

From *Antigone*
Sophocles

Prologue

SCENE: Before the palace of Creon, king of Thebes. A central double door,
and two lateral doors. A platform extends the length of the facade, and
from this platform three steps lead down into the "orchestra," or
chorus-ground.

TIME: Dawn of the day after the defeat of the **Argive** army in their
assault on Thebes.

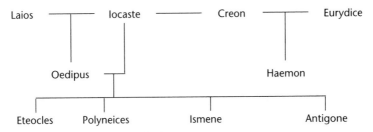

Figure 7 • Royal House of Thebes

Antigone and Ismene enter from the central door of the palace.

ANTIGONE: Ismene, **dear** sister,
   You would think that we had already suffered enough
   For the curse on Oedipus:
   I cannot imagine any **grief**
   That you and I have not gone through. And now— 5
   Have they told you of the new **decree** of our King Creon?

ISMENE: I have heard nothing: I know
   That two sisters lost two brothers, a double death
   In a single hour; and I know that the Argive army
   Fled in the night; but beyond this, nothing. 10

ANTIGONE: I thought so. And that is why I wanted you
   To come out here with me. There is something we must do.

ISMENE: Why do you speak so strangely?

ANTIGONE: Listen, Ismene:
   Creon **buried** our brother Eteocles 15
   With military honors, gave him a soldier's funeral,
   And it was right that he should; but Polyneices,
   Who fought as bravely and died as miserably,—
   They say that Creon has sworn
   No one shall bury him, no one **mourn** for him, 20
   But his body must lie in the fields, a sweet treasure
   For **carrion birds** to find as they search for food.
   That is what they say, and our good Creon is coming here
   To announce it publicly; and the penalty—
   Stoning to death in the public square! 25
                              There it is,
   And now you can prove what you are:
   A true sister, or a traitor to your family.

ISMENE: Antigone, you are mad! What could I possibly do?

ANTIGONE: You must decide whether you will help me or not.   30

ISMENE: I do not understand you. Help you in what?

ANTIGONE: Ismene, I am going to bury him. Will you come?

ISMENE: Bury him! You have just said the new law forbids it.

ANTIGONE: He is my brother. And he is your brother, too.

ISMENE: But think of the danger! Think what Creon will do!   35

ANTIGONE: Creon is not strong enough to stand in my way.

ISMENE: Ah sister!
   Oedipus died, everyone hating him
   For what his own search brought to light, his eyes
   Ripped out by his own hand; and Iocaste died,   40
   His mother and wife at once: she twisted the **cords**
   That **strangled** her life; and our two brothers died,
   Each killed by the other's sword. And we are left:
   But oh, Antigone,
   Think how much more terrible than these   45
   Our own death would be if we should go against Creon
   And do what he has **forbidden!** We are only women,
   We cannot fight with men, Antigone!
   The law is strong, we must give in to the law
   In this thing, and in worse. I beg the Dead   50
   To forgive me, but I am helpless: I must yield
   To those in authority. And I think it is dangerous business
   To be always **meddling.**

ANTIGONE: If that is what you think,
   I should not want you, even if you asked to come.   55
   You have made your choice, you can be what you want to be.
   But I will bury him; and if I must die,
   I say that this crime is holy: I shall lie down
   With him in death, and I shall be as dear
   To him as he to me.   60
                    It is the dead,
   Not the living, who make the longest demands:
   We die forever. . . .
                    You may do as you like,
   Since apparently the laws of the gods mean nothing to you.   65

ISMENE: They mean a great deal to me; but I have no strength
   To break laws that were made for the public good.

ANTIGONE: That must be your excuse, I suppose. But as for me,
   I will bury the brother I love.

IsMENE:　　　　　　　　　　　Antigone,　　　　　　　　　　70
　　I am so afraid for you!

ANTIGONE:　　　　　　　You need not be:
　　You have yourself to consider, after all.

IsMENE: But no one must hear of this, you must tell no one!
　　I will keep it a secret, I promise!　　　　　　　　75

ANTIGONE:　　　　　　　　　O tell it! Tell everyone!
　　Think how they'll hate you when it all comes out
　　If they learn that you knew about it all the time!

IsMENE: So **fiery**! You should be cold with fear.

ANTIGONE: Perhaps. But I am doing only what I must.　　80

IsMENE: But can you do it? I say you cannot.

ANTIGONE: Very well, when my strength gives out,
　　I shall do no more.

IsMENE: Impossible things should not be tried at all.

ANTIGONE: Go away, Ismene:　　　　　　　　　　　85
　　I shall be hating you soon, and the dead will too,
　　For your words are hateful. Leave me my foolish plan:
　　I am not afraid of the danger; if it means death,
　　It will not be the worst of deaths—death without honor.

IsMENE: Go then, if you feel you must.　　　　　　　90
　　You are unwise,
　　But a loyal friend indeed to those who love you.

"Ode to Man"

CHORUS: Numberless are the world's wonders, but none　　Strophe 1
　　More wonderful than man; the stormgray sea
　　Yields to his **prows**, the huge **crests** bear him high;
　　Earth, holy and inexhaustible, is **graven**
　　With the shining **furrows** where his **plows** have gone
　　Year after year, the timeless labor of **stallions**.

　　The lightboned birds and beasts that **cling** to cover,　　Antistrophe 1
　　The **lithe** fish lighting their **reaches** of dim water,
　　All are taken, tamed in the net of his mind;
　　The lion on the hill, the wild horse windy-maned,
　　Resign to him; and his **blunt** yoke has broken
　　The sultry shoulders of the mountain bull.

　　Words also, and thought as rapid as air,　　Strophe 2
　　He fashions to his good use; **statecraft** is his,

Figure 8 • Plan of an ancient Greek theater

And his the skill that **deflects** the arrows of snow,
The spears of winter rain: from every wind
He has made himself secure—from all but one:
In the late wind of death he cannot stand.
O clear intelligence, force beyond all measure!   Antistrophe 2
O fate of man, working both good and evil!
When the laws are kept, how proudly his city stands!
When the laws are broken, what of his city then?
Never may the **anarchic** man find rest at my **hearth**,
Never be it said that my thoughts are his thoughts.

Vocabulary

PROLOGUE

*Argive *(adj.)*   from the Greek city of Argos
bury *(v.)*   to put into the earth
*carrion birds *(n.)*   birds that eat dead flesh
cord *(n.)*   rope

*Denotes low-frequency word.

dear *(adj.)*   precious; loved
decree *(n.)*   formal decision made by an authority
fiery *(adj.)*   full of emotion
flee (fled, fled) *(v.)*   to run away
forbid (forbade, forbidden) *(v.)*   to command against
grief *(n.)*   deep feeling caused by loss; sorrow
meddle *(v.)*   to be interested in something that is not one's concern
mourn *(v.)*   to feel or express grief or sorrow
rip out *(v.)*   to tear out
strangle *(v.)*   to choke

"ODE TO MAN"

*anarchic *(adj.)*   causing political disorder
blunt *(adj.)*   not sharp
cling *(v.)*   to hold on tightly to
crest *(n.)*   top of a wave
deflect *(v.)*   to turn from course
furrow *(n.)*   line in the earth made by a plow
*graven *(adj.)*   cut; carved
hearth *(n.)*   floor of a fireplace; home
lithe *(adj.)*   very flexible and graceful
plow *(n.)*   agricultural tool used to turn over the earth
prow *(n.)*   front part of a ship
reach *(n.)*   expanse; stretch
resign *(v.)*   to submit
stallion *(n.)*   male horse
statecraft *(n.)*   art of conducting state affairs

Activities

1. Looking at the Prologue, make notes in your journal about the characters or personalities of the two sisters, Ismene and Antigone. How are they different?

2. With your study group, discuss the meaning of each stanza (group of lines) in "Ode to Man." What kind of imagery does Sophocles use? Write a brief summary of the entire ode in your journal.

3. An ode is a poem that praises a person or an object. What qualities about human beings does Sophocles admire in "Ode to Man"? What are human beings capable of controlling? What can they not control?

4. How is "Ode to Man," especially the last stanza, connected to the conflict presented in the Prologue? What kind of law is Antigone breaking? What kind of law is Creon breaking? With your study group, discuss the importance of each of the two kinds of law. Organize and record your ideas in your journal.

5. What is the role of religion in this drama? What is the role of myth? Why would the Greeks act these elements out?

6. Write an essay comparing and contrasting Antigone and Ismene.

7. Based on the discussion and your journal notes, write your own essay comparing and contrasting the law that Antigone believes in and the kind of law that Creon makes. In your essay, evaluate the importance of each.

For Further Reading

Burkert, Walter. *Greek Religion*. Cambridge, MA: Harvard UP, 1985.

Grant, Michael. *The Classical Greeks*. New York: Scribner's, 1989.

Hogan, James C. *A Commentary on the Plays of Sophocles*. Carbondale: Southern Illinois UP, 1991.

Ley, Graham. *A Short Introduction to the Ancient Greek Theater*. Chicago: U of Chicago P, 1991.

Figure 9   •   Map of East Asia

5

From "Red Thread Maiden"

Yuan Chiao (late ninth century)
Fiction: Short Story

Background

Elizabeth Te-Chen Wang, translator and editor of *Ladies of the T'ang*, took this story from a collection of short stories by Yuan Chiao. Not much is known about the author, but she seems to have been an educated lady of the court in northern China. Unlike most popular storytellers of her day, Yuan Chiao was able to write down her stories as well as recite them. "Red Thread Maiden" reflects the civil strife during the T'ang dynasty (618–906). The story is strongly influenced by the religious and ethical concerns of Buddhism, the religion brought from India, and of the native Chinese Confucianism.

The T'ang dynasty was the golden age of Chinese poetry. A well-known collection of the best poets, *Poems from the T'ang Dynasty*, became a school literary text and has been translated several times into English.

During the T'ang dynasty, foreign trade increased and new ideas were brought to China. In particular, monks from India and Central Asia strengthened the influence of Buddhism. Buddhist religious relics appeared, and soon Chinese men and women were retiring to live in monasteries apart from the strife of the courts. Although efforts were made to control Buddhism, its effects on Chinese life were permanent.

The T'ang dynasty was weakened by a rebellion led by the Empress Wu in 683. However, the T'ang were restored to power in 705. A second major rebellion occurred in 755 when the northern Chinese general An Lu-Shan fought against the emperor. Although An Lu-Shan was defeated in 763, the T'ang dynasty was undermined and later lost most of its control over northeast China. The political difficulties of the T'ang are depicted in the story of "Red Thread Maiden."

Pre-Reading Activities

1. Civil war or other serious conflict may occur anywhere, at any time. Discuss with your group or class how people might try to resolve such conflict. What role might women play in solving the conflict?
2. With your group or class, discuss what you know about reincarnation. Which religions do you think might consider it an important concept?

Key Terms

These terms are important for the mini-lecture and class discussion.

An Lu-Shan Rebellion
   (755–763 C.E.)
Buddhism/Buddhist
civil service
Confucian Five Classics
Confucius (551–479 B.C.E.)/
   Confucianism

dynasty
humanism
monastery
Second Imperial Period
T'ang dynasty (618–906 C.E.)
warlord

From "Red Thread Maiden"
Yuan Chiao

In the household of General Hsueh Sung, the military governor   1
of Luchow, lived the maid Red Thread. Because Red Thread was **well grounded** in the classics as well as in letter writing, Hsueh appointed her as his personal secretary. . . . But he was particularly fond of her for another reason. She was good at music and could tell the emotional state of the player by listening to the tune of a musical instrument.

One day General Hsueh gave a feast for his staff members   2
and the soldiers under his command. Red Thread was ordered to be present. While she was enjoying the musical performance, she noticed something wrong with the drummer.

"Something sad is on the drummer's mind," she remarked, 3
"for the tune of the drum is sorrowful."

Hsueh Sung also understood music; he agreed with Red 4
Thread and said, "I think so." He then summoned the drummer and
questioned him.

The drummer was frightened. "My wife died last night," 5
he **murmured**, with tears in his eyes. "Since I dare not ask for
leave, I cannot control my **grief** when I beat the drum. Please forgive me if I have offended Your Excellency." Hsueh immediately
gave him leave to go to the funeral.

It was during the period of Chih Teh, right after the rebel- 6
lion led by An Lu-Shan, and everything was not yet restored to order. Along the **Yangtze** and **Yellow rivers** there still existed unrest
and fighting, for the warlords did not trust one another and constantly made trouble. In addition to General Hsueh Sung, the most
powerful and notable military governors were General Tien Cheng-
tze of Weipo and General Ling-Hu Chang of Huachow.

Although the Emperor had put Hsueh Sung in charge of the 7
newly organized Chaoyi Regiment with orders to set up his headquarters in Fuyang in order to control the whole of Shantung
province, it was still doubtful whether there could be peaceful coexis-
tence between the three **rampant** warlords. To **pacify** them the
Emperor had arranged for the daughter of Hsueh Sung to wed the
son of Tien Cheng-tze, and for Hsueh's son to marry the daughter of
Ling-Hu Chang. Messengers and presents were sent back and forth,
and there was **superficial** harmony among the three states.

Then Tien Cheng-tze fell ill with a kind of sickness caused by 8
the bad weather. He felt worse during the summertime. "If I can
change my office with Hsueh Sung and move to Shantung, where
the weather is much cooler," he thought to himself, "I probably can
cure my disease and live a few years longer." With this in mind, he
conscripted three thousand soldiers, ten times braver than the ones
he already had, and gave them special training. He paid them well
and called them Outside Guards. Each night he ordered three hundred of them to take turns guarding his residence. A lucky date was
chosen; he intended to move to Luchow by any means. This meant
that an open conflict would occur between Weipo and Luchow.

When Hsueh Sung heard of the intention of General Tien, he 9
was surprised and worried, not because he did not want to have a
fight with his **kinsman**, but because the troops he had were getting
old and could not compete with the fresh soldiers of the Outside
Guards. He did not know what to do except to worry all day long.

It was midnight. The gates of the headquarters were **bolted**.   10
Hseuh Sung, cane in hand, was **pacing agitatedly** along the **corridors** of the courtyard. He had no other attendant besides Red
Thread. "Why is it that Your Lordship has not slept or eaten well for
the entire past month?" asked Red Thread. "Is it due to something
from the neighboring state?"

"A big affair that concerns the safety of the whole country is   11
something you cannot understand," answered Hsueh Sung.

"Though I am a **bondmaid**, perhaps I know how to lift the   12
burden from the mind of Your Lordship."

Hsueh Sung confided the whole story to her. "I inherited this   13
command from my father and would like to keep it till the end of my
life and bestow it on my son. If I lose this, I will lose everything."

"It is a simple matter and should not worry Your Lordship,"   14
said Red Thread. "Just let me go to Weipo to make a **reconnaissance**.
I shall leave here at the first **watch** and come back by the third.
Please prepare a good horse and a friendly letter and wait till my return."

. . . Red Thread then went back to her own chamber and   15
changed her costume. She wound her long hair into a knot and
pinned it up with a golden hairpin made into the shape of a **phoenix**
and covered her head with a red scarf. **Donning** an embroidered
purple robe and a pair of black shoes, she hung around her waist a
dagger that bore the sign of a dragon. On her forehead she wrote
the name of the god Tai Yi to guard her from evil spirits. She saluted
Hsueh Sung and at once disappeared.

Hsueh Sung walked into his room and, closing the door, sat   16
down in tense silence, with his back to the candlelight. He drank a
dozen cups of wine, but felt neither drunk nor sleepy. As he was
waiting in suspense, he heard the distant sound of the morning horn.
A sudden breeze rustled by and a leaf fell from a dewy tree. Before
he had time to wonder what it was, Red Thread was already standing
in front of him. Hsueh Sung was in **rapture**.

"Was everything all right?" asked he.   17
"How dare I fail to carry out a mission for Your Lordship?"   18
"Did you do any killing?"   19
"No, I only took a golden box from beneath General Tien's   20
pillow."

She gave the golden box to Hsueh Sung and then described   21
her trip.

"About three-quarters of an hour before midnight I arrived at   22
General Tien's residence. I passed through several courtyards and fi-

nally reached his bedroom. His Outside Guards were sleeping in the corridors, snoring like thunder. Other soldiers were pacing in the courtyard so vigilant that a wisp of breeze would start them shooting. But I made no noise as I opened the door and approached General Tien's bed. When I lifted the bed curtains, I saw old General Tien sound asleep on a rhinoceros-horn pillow, with his chest uncovered. His hair was bound up in a piece of yellow silk. Beside his pillow there lay a sword with seven stars carved upon it, and in front of the sword there lay a golden box containing the eight characters of his horoscope and the name of the god of the North Pole.

". . . All of General Tien's bodyguards and servants were   23
getting drowsy. Some rested their heads against the screens. Others leaned on their weapons and covered themselves with hand towels. I pulled the hairpin from one and touched the clothes of another, but they all slept like sick men or drunkards. Finally, I took the golden box from beside General Tien's pillow and left the city of Wei by the west gate. After I had walked two hundred **li** away, I looked back and saw the bronze casement towering among the clouds above the Chang River, which runs eastward. It was beautiful to see the morning breeze beginning to stir the grass and flowers of the wild meadows and the declining moon half hidden by the tall trees.

"I was so glad to be back that I entirely forgot my worries   24
and the fatigue of the **strenuous** trip. It makes me feel happy to be of a little service to you to repay some of your kindness. To show my gratitude to you is the main reason that I ran the risk of entering an enemy state, passing five or six cities, and completing a trip of about seven hundred li in three watches' time. I did this to lessen your grief, so I have no complaint."

Hsueh Sung hurriedly **dispatched** a messenger on the horse   25
that he had prepared, giving him the letter that he had written. The letter was for Governor Tien, and it read:

"Last night a guest came from Your Lordship's headquarters   26
and presented me with a golden box which he said he took from beneath your pillow. As your humble relative, how can I accept such a gift which is so precious and important to you? Therefore, I am sending it back with my best regards."

The messenger galloped as fast as he could. When he reached   27
Weipo at daybreak, he found General Tien's headquarters in great confusion searching for the missing golden box. Everyone was under suspicion. The messenger hammered on the gate with his horsewhip and asked for the governor. Tien Cheng-tze immediately came out and, upon receiving the box, was terrified to think that someone

could steal anything from beneath his pillow. The man who dared to do this must be of **unsurpassable** courage and skill, and could easily have cut his head off. He decided that he had better be loyal to General Hsueh from that time on, since the latter possessed such a magically **endowed** knight.

Governor Tien therefore invited the messenger to stay in his residence, treating him to a big feast and giving him many gifts. Next day, upon sending the messenger back, he presented to Governor Hsueh thirty thousand pieces of fine silk, two hundred good horses, and many other presents. He also wrote an exceeding polite letter to Governor Hsueh: 28

"My life was at the mercy of a man from your state last night. As a relative, you have been very kind to me. How can I do anything that might cause you great concern? Please suspect me no more. The so-called Outside Guards were trained to deal with robbers and bandits only. Now I have discharged them and sent them back to their farms in order to show you my cooperation. From now on I shall be at your service. If you care to give any orders, I shall follow your carriage to carry them out; and if you ever come to my **humble** state, I shall stand by to watch your horse for you." 29

Thus the two governors were **reconciled**. Greetings were exchanged frequently, and the tension eased between the south and north sides of the Yellow River. 30

A month or so later Red Thread asked for **leave**. "You were **reared** in my house," exclaimed Hsueh Sung. "Where can you go? Moreover, you have done me a great favor and I depend on you for my safety. How can I let you go?" 31

But Red Thread told him: "I was a man in my previous life, an herb doctor who wandered from village to village to cure people with prescriptions from the book of Shen Lung. One day I ran across a pregnant woman suffering from a kind of **dropsy**. I gave her some wine made of a certain kind of flower that caused her death and the death of her unborn twins. My mistake in killing three persons with one dose was reported to the king of the underworld, and as punishment I was reincarnated as a woman in this life. I was moreover punished by being born a lowbred maid with an ill star of ability to act like a burglar. It was fortunate that I was sold to your house. For nineteen years I have been so well treated that I have even tired of the soft dresses that you give me and the delicious food I have eaten day after day. You have been exceedingly kind to me. I was even honored by being appointed your personal secretary. 32

"Because our country had just survived the **calamity** of re- 33 bellion, I hated to see the warlords make trouble again and endanger the peace and safety of the whole nation. So I went to Weipo to give General Tien a warning. I did that to repay your kindness and to avoid a civil war which would no doubt destroy thousands of lives. My little deed of saving two states from destruction and warning the warlords of the cost of an open conflict has made it possible for the military strategists to set their minds at ease. As a woman, I feel that I have done enough to **redeem** the crime I committed in my previous life, and now it is time for me to **retreat** from this world. I hope to become a man again and live an immortal life."

. . . Seeing it was **futile** to persuade her to stay, Hsueh Sung   34
gave her a big farewell party, with all the high officers invited. In the midst of the elaborate food and toasts, Hsueh Sung asked Lung Chao-yang, a guest and also a poet, to compose a poem for him to sing to Red Thread. The poem became very famous. It runs as follows:

> From the orchid boat comes the sad
>   water-chestnut song—
> Standing on the tall tower, everyone
>   grieves over the parting.
> Like Fairy Lo flying to the clouds, you
>   now leave,
> Boundless is the blue sky and the water
>   runs on forever.

Hsueh Sung felt the weight of great sadness after he had sung   35
the song. Red Thread wept. Because she did not want to **tarry** any longer, she made an excuse that she was drunk and must retire. She saluted the general and the guests and left. No one ever saw her again.

Vocabulary

agitatedly *(adv.)*   with rapid or violent action
bolt *(v.)*   to close with locks
*bondmaid *(n.)*   woman bound to service without wages; slave
calamity *(n.)*   disaster
conscript *(v.)*   to force into military service
corridor *(n.)*   passageway into which rooms open
dagger *(n.)*   sharp-pointed knife for stabbing

*Denotes low-frequency word.

dispatch *(v.)*   to send off with speed, especially on official business
*don *(v.)*   to put on
*dropsy *(n.)*   abnormal fluid in body tissues; edema
endowed *(adj.)*   gifted
futile *(adj.)*   serving no useful purpose
grief *(n.)*   sorrow
humble *(adj.)*   low-ranking
*kinsman *(n.)*   male relative (in this case by marriage)
*leave *(n.)*   permission to leave
*li *(n.)*   Chinese measure of distance, about one-third of a mile
murmur *(v.)*   to speak in a low voice or unclearly
pace *(v.)*   to walk with a measured step
pacify *(v.)*   to settle; to restore to a peaceful state
*phoenix *(n.)*   mythological Chinese bird of good fortune
rampant *(adj.)*   wild; without restraint
rapture *(n.)*   state of overwhelming emotion
rear *(v.)*   to raise; bring up
reconcile *(v.)*   to restore to harmony
*reconnaissance *(n.)*   preliminary inspection
redeem *(v.)*   to make amends for; to atone for
retreat *(v.)*   to withdraw
strenuous *(adj.)*   calling for energy or stamina
superficial *(adj.)*   on the surface; without substance
*tarry *(v.)*   to delay
unsurpassable *(adj.)*   not to be exceeded
watch *(n.)*   period of guard duty
well grounded *(adj.)*   having a firm foundation
Yangtze River *(prop. n.)*   the longest and largest river in China; begins in Tsinghai province and runs to the East China Sea north of the city of Shanghai
Yellow River *(prop. n.)*   the second-longest river in China, nicknamed "China's Sorrow" because of its periodic and devastating floods. The lower part of the Yellow River was the site of China's earliest civilization. Loyang, capital of the T'ang dynasty, is located on its banks.

Activities

1.   Why was Red Thread born? How does she pay her debt?
2.   With your study group or class, find evidence that magic or the supernatural is important in the story. Make notes in your journal and compare your answers with the answers of other members of your class.

*Denotes low-frequency word.

3. Look at the details of the story and make notes in your journal about the cultural values or beliefs that are important to the Chinese of the T'ang dynasty. For example, how is the role of women viewed? Discuss these beliefs with your class.

4. Based on your notes and class discussion, write an essay on the importance of the balance of physical strength with emotional sensitivity in "Red Thread Maiden."

5. Based on your notes and discussion, write an essay on the cultural values of the T'ang Chinese court.

For Further Reading

Bary, William de, et al, eds. *Sources of Chinese Tradition*. New York: Columbia UP, 1960.

Grousset, René. *The Rise and Splendour of the Chinese Empire*. Berkeley: U of California P, 1953.

Meskill, John, ed. *An Introduction to Chinese Civilization*. New York: Columbia UP, 1960.

Moore, Charles A. *The Chinese Mind: Essentials of Chinese Philosophy and Culture*. Honolulu: U of Hawaii P, 1986.

Shimer, Dorothy Blair, ed. *Rice Bowl Women*. New York: Meridian, 1982.

Figure 10 • Map of England, France, Germany, and the English Channel

6

"Bisclavret" from *The Lais of Marie de France*

Marie de France (late twelfth century)
Fiction: Short Story

Background

Little is known about the life of the medieval author called Marie de France. Immensely popular in French and English aristocratic courts during her lifetime, Marie de France composed religious pieces in Latin but is most remembered for her secular literature. Marie wrote these pieces in Old French, the language spoken from the ninth century C.E. until Modern French evolved in the sixteenth century. Old French was also the language of high culture in the English court after the French Norman Conquest of England in 1066.

The Lais, a collection of 12 short poems, tells of the adventures of noblemen and noblewomen as they follow or disobey the principles of courtly love. Marie herself says that as her source material she used lais from Brittany, an area in northwestern France where a Celtic language is spoken. These Breton lais were traditionally adventures of ancient origin told in verse and set to music. Whether Marie heard these lais in Old French or in Celtic is not clear.

The subject of the lai "Bisclavret" is one that fascinated medieval Europeans: the power to transform oneself or another into a wolf by the use of magic. In the tale, this strange phenomenon tests the courtly conventions of the relationship between husband and wife and between noble and feudal lord.

Pre-Reading Activities

1. With your study group, discuss what you think is the purpose of literature. Should it merely entertain, or should it teach a moral lesson?

2. Imagine what life was like in Europe 800 years ago. In your journal list your ideas about why storytelling would be important for people living at that time. Discuss your ideas with your group.

Key Terms

Breton/Brittany   Middle Ages/medieval
chivalry   Old French
courtly love   piety
feudal system   Provence/Provençal
folklore   secular
knights and ladies   vernacular
lai (lay)   werewolf
loyalty

"Bisclavret"
Marie de France

In my effort to compose lais I do not wish to omit "Bisclavret". . . . In days gone by . . . many men turned into werewolves and went to live in the woods. A werewolf is a **ferocious** beast which, when possessed by this madness, devours men, causes great damage and **dwells** in vast forests. I leave such matters for the moment, for I wish to tell you about Bisclavret. [1–14]*

In Brittany there lived a **baron** whom I have heard greatly   2
praised. He was a good and handsome knight who conducted himself nobly. He was one of his lord's closest advisers and was well loved by all his neighbors. As his wedded wife he had a woman who was worthy and attractive in appearance. He loved her and she returned his love. But one thing caused her great worry: Each week he was absent for three full days without her knowing what became of him or where he went. . . .

*Line numbers refer to original French text.

Figure 11 • Medieval werewolf, an imaginary wolf-man

One day, when he had returned home in high spirits, she   3
questioned him: "Lord," she said, "my dear, sweet love, I would
gladly ask you something, if only I dared; but there is nothing I fear
more than your anger." [15–35]

When he heard this, he embraced her, drew her towards him   4
and kissed her. "Lady," he said, "come, ask your question! There is
nothing you can ask which I shall not tell you, if I know the answer." "In faith," she said, "I am relieved to hear this. Lord, I am so
fraught with anxiety the days you are apart from me, my heart is
so heavy and I have such a fear of losing you that I shall surely die
shortly from this unless I soon get help. Please tell me where you go,
[and] what becomes of you. . . . I think you must have a lover
and, if this is so, you are doing wrong." "Lady," he said, "in God's
name, have mercy on me! If I tell you this, great harm will come

to me, for as a result, I shall lose your love and destroy myself."
[36–56]

When the lady heard what he said, she thought it was no   5
laughing matter. She questioned him repeatedly and **coaxed** him so
persuasively that he told her his story, keeping nothing secret. "Lady,
I become a werewolf: I enter the **vast** forest and live in the deepest
part of the wood where I feed off the **prey** I can capture." When he
had related everything to her, she asked him whether he undressed
or remained clothed. "Lady," he said, "I go about completely naked."
"Tell me, in the name of God, where do you leave your clothes?"
"That I will not tell you, for if I lost them and were discovered in that
state, I should remain a werewolf forever. No one would be able to
help me until they were returned to me. That is why I do not wish
this to be known." [57–79]

"Lord," the lady replied to him, "I love you more than the   6
whole world. You must not hide anything from me. . . . That would
not seem like true love. What have I done wrong? What sin have I
committed that you should doubt me in any way? Do tell me—you
will be acting wisely." She **tormented** . . . him so much that he
could not do otherwise but tell her.

"Lady," he said, "beside the wood, near the path I follow,   7
stands an old chapel. . . . There beneath a bush is a broad stone,
hollowed out in the center, in which I put my clothes until I return
home." The lady heard this remarkable revelation and her face became flushed with fear. She was greatly alarmed by the story, and began to consider various means of parting from him, as she no longer
wished to lie with him. [80–102]

She sent a messenger to **summon** a knight who lived in the   8
region and who had loved her for a long time, wooed her **ardently**
and served her generously. She had never loved him or promised
him her affection but now she told him what was on her mind.
"Friend," she said, "rejoice; without further delay I grant you that
which has tormented you; never again will you encounter any refusal. I offer you my love and my body; make me your mistress."

He thanked her warmly and accepted her pledge, whereupon   9
she received his oath and told him of her husband and what became
of him. She described the path he took to the forest and sent him for
her husband's clothes. Thus was Bisclavret betrayed and wronged by
his wife. Because he was often missing, everyone thought that this
time he had gone away for good. They searched . . . for him a long
while but no trace of him was found. . . . Then the knight married
the lady he had loved for so long. [103–34]

A whole year passed by until one day the king went hunting   10
and headed straight for the forest in which Bisclavret was living.
When the hounds were unleashed they came upon Bisclavret and
the dogs and hunters spent the whole day in pursuit until they were
just about to capture him, tear him to pieces and destroy him. As
soon as he saw the king he ran up to him and begged for mercy. He
took hold of his **stirrup** and kissed his foot and his leg. The king saw
him and was filled with dread. He summoned all his companions.
"Lords," he said, "come forward! See the marvellous way this beast
humbles itself before me! It has the intelligence of a human and is
pleading for mercy. Drive back all the dogs and see that no one
strikes it! The beast possesses understanding and intelligence. Hurry!
Let us depart. I shall place the creature under my protection, for I
shall hunt no more today." [135–60]

The king then left with Bisclavret following him. He kept very   11
close to the king, as he did not want to be separated from him. . . .
The king, who took him straight to his castle, was delighted and
overjoyed. . . . He considered the wolf to be a great wonder and
loved it dearly, commanding all his people to guard it well for love of
him and not to do it any harm. None of them was to strike it and
plenty of food and water must be provided each day for it. His men
were happy to look after the creature and each day it would sleep
amongst the knights, just by the king. It was loved by everyone and
so noble and gentle a beast was it that it never attempted to cause
any harm. Wherever the king might go, it never wanted to be left behind. . . . It showed clearly that it loved him. [161–84]

Now hear what happened next. The king held court and all   12
his barons and those who held **fiefs** from him were summoned so
that they could help him celebrate the festival. . . . Amongst them,
richly and elegantly attired, was the knight who had married
Bisclavret's wife. He did not realize and would never have suspected
that Bisclavret was so close by. As soon as he arrived at the palace,
Bisclavret caught sight of the knight and **sped** towards him, sinking
his teeth into him and dragging him down. . . . He would soon
have done the knight serious harm if the king had not called him and
threatened him with a stick. On two occasions that day he attempted to bite him. Many people were greatly astonished at this for
never before had he shown signs of such behavior towards anyone
he had seen. Throughout the household it was remarked that he
would not have done it without good reason. The knight had
wronged him somehow or other, for he **was bent on** revenge. . . .
[185–218]

Not long afterwards, as I understand it, the king, who was   13
wise and courtly, went into the forest where Bisclavret had been discovered. Bisclavret accompanied him and on the way home that
night the king took **lodging** in that region. Bisclavret's wife learnt of
this and, dressing herself elegantly, went next day to speak to the
king, taking an expensive present for him. When Bisclavret saw her
approach, no one could restrain him. He dashed towards her like a
madman. Just hear how successfully he took his revenge. He tore the
nose right off her face. What worse punishment could he have
inflicted on her?

From all sides he was threatened and was on the point of being   14
torn to pieces, when a wise man said to the king: "Lord, listen to me.
This beast has lived with . . . us over a long period. . . . Never before has he touched a soul or committed a hostile act, except against
this lady here. By the faith I owe you, he has some **grudge** against
her and also her husband. She is the wife of the knight you used to
love so dearly and who has been missing for a long time without our
knowing what became of him. Question the lady to see if she will tell
you why the beast hates her. Make her tell you, if she knows! We
have witnessed many marvels happening in Brittany." [219–60]

The king accepted his advice. Holding the knight, he took the   15
lady away and **subjected** her to torture. Pain and fear combined
made her **reveal** everything about her husband; how she had betrayed him and taken his clothes, about his account of what happened, what became of him and where he went. Since his clothes
had been taken he had not been seen in the region. She was quite
convinced that the beast was Bisclavret. The king asked her for the
clothes and . . . made her bring them and return them to
Bisclavret. When they were placed before him, Bisclavret took no notice of them. The man who gave the advice earlier called to the king:
"Lord, you are not acting properly: Nothing would **induce** him to
put on his clothing in front of you or change his animal form. You do
not realize the importance of this; it is most **humiliating** for him.
Take him into your bedchamber and bring him the clothes. Let us
leave him there for a while and we shall soon see if he turns into a
man." [261–92]

The king himself led the way and closed all the doors on the wolf.   16
After a while he returned, taking two barons with him. All three entered the room. They found the knight sleeping on the king's own
bed. The king ran forward to embrace him, and kissed him many
times. It was not long before he restored his land to him; he gave him
more than I can tell and banished the woman from the country, exil-

ing her from the region. The man for whom she betrayed her husband went with her. She had a good many children who were thereafter recognizable by their appearance. Many of the women in the family, I tell you truly, were born without noses and lived noseless. [293–314]

The adventure you have heard actually took place, do not doubt   17
it. The lai was **composed** about Bisclavret to be remembered for ever more. [315-18]

Vocabulary

ardently *(adv.)*   with intense feeling
*baron *(n.)*   nobleman
*be bent on *(v.)*   to be determined or strongly inclined [to have]
coax *(v.)*   to urge gently
compose *(v.)*   to create by mental or artistic labor
dwell *(v.)*   to live as a resident
ferocious *(adj.)*   given to extreme fierceness and unrestrained violence
*fief *(n.)*   feudal estate
*fraught [with] *(adj.)*   full [of]
grudge *(n.)*   feeling of deep resentment or ill will
humiliating *(adj.)*   extremely destructive to one's self-respect
induce *(v.)*   to persuade; to influence
inflict *(v.)*   to carry out by physical assault; to impose
lodging *(n.)*   temporary place to stay for the night
prey *(n.)*   any animal hunted or killed for food
reveal *(v.)*   to make publicly known something that was secret or hidden
speed (sped, sped) *(v.)*   to move quickly
*stirrup *(n.)*   part of a saddle for the rider's foot
subject *(v.)*   to force someone to endure something unpleasant
summon *(v.)*   to call forth; to demand the presence of
threaten *(v.)*   to express one's intention of hurting or punishing
torment *(v.)*   to cause severe distress of body or mind
vast *(adj.)*   very great in size

Activities

1. As a character, Bisclavret is presented as a model of chivalry. Make notes in your journal of his courtly behavior. How is he rewarded? Discuss your ideas with your class.

*Denotes low-frequency word.

2. The story "Bisclavret" focuses on fidelity, or faithfulness, an important concept in the feudal system. What kinds of fidelity play a role in the story? What happens to those who are unfaithful?

3. Based on your notes and class discussion, write a description of courtly life in the Middle Ages.

4. With a partner or alone, note the portions of the story where Marie de France uses her imagination to entertain her audience. Write a summary of the use of the fantastic (the not-real) in "Bisclavret."

5. Based on your notes and discussion, write an essay on "Bisclavret" as a fictional story that both entertains and teaches a moral lesson.

For Further Reading

Clifford, Paula. *Marie de France*. London: Grant and Culter, 1982.

Marie de France. *The Lais of Marie de France*. Trans. and intro. by Glynn S. Burgess and Keith Busby. London: Penguin, 1986.

Morewedge, Rosmarie Thee, ed. *The Role of Woman in the Middle Ages*. Albany: State U of New York P, 1975.

Rose, Mary Beth, ed. *Women in the Middle Ages and the Renaissance: Literary and Historical Perspectives*. Syracuse: Syracuse UP, 1986.

Wilson, Katherina M., ed. *Medieval Women Writers*. Athens: U of Georgia P, 1984.

CHAPTER 7

From "The Miller's Tale" from *The Canterbury Tales*

Geoffrey Chaucer (1340?–1400)

Oral Tradition and Poetry: Verse Narrative

Background

The most important author writing in English in the European Middle Ages was Geoffrey Chaucer. The son of a London merchant, Chaucer was sent to the house of a noble family where he received a classical education including the study of French, Italian, and Latin. Chaucer's educational experiences served as major sources for his writing. His travel to the European continent also provided material for his work. The influence of these sources can be seen in his most famous effort, *The Canterbury Tales*.

Chaucer frames his tales in verse as a story of 29 men and women making a religious pilgrimage to the tomb of St. Thomas à Becket at Canterbury Cathedral in England. The pilgrims represent the upper middle class of medieval society. The travelers compete in telling stories to entertain their companions during the trip. In his tale, the Miller parodies, or makes fun of, the previous story of courtly love told by a knight.

Pre-Reading Activities

1. With your study group, discuss why religious pilgrims might tell funny stories to pass the time. What does this say about the character of the pilgrims?
2. What kinds of things make people laugh?

Key Terms

These terms and concepts are important for understanding *The Canterbury Tales*. They will be used in the mini-lecture and in class discussion.

Absalon	Greek and Roman classics
bawdy	King Henry II (ruled 1154–1189)
biblical	Middle English
Boccaccio, Giovanni (1313–1375)	moral
Canterbury Cathedral	parody
Cato	pilgrim/pilgrimage
comedy	ribald
couplet	St. Thomas à Becket (1118–1170)
Decameron	satire
fabliau/fabliaux	slapstick
framed narrative	

From "The Miller's Tale"
Geoffrey Chaucer

Some time ago there was a rich old **codger**
Who lived in Oxford and who took a **lodger**.
The fellow was a carpenter by trade,
His lodger a poor student who had made
Some studies in the arts, but all his fancy   5
Turned to astrology and **geomancy**,
And he could deal with certain propositions
And make a forecast under some conditions
About the likelihood of drought or showers
For those who asked at favorable hours. . . .   10
This lad was known as Nicholas the **Gallant**,

Figure 12 • **Pilgrims on the road to Canterbury** *(The Granger Collection)*

And making love in secret was his talent. . . .
He rented a small chamber in the **kip**
All by himself without companionship. . . .
He had an **astrolabe** to match his art 15
And calculating counters laid apart. . . .
This carpenter had married a new wife
Not long before, and loved her more than life.
She was a girl of eighteen years of age.
Jealous he was and kept her in the cage, 20
For he was old and she was wild and young;
He thought himself quite likely to be **stung**.
He might have known, were Cato on his shelf,
A man should marry someone like himself;

A man should pick an equal for his mate.   25
Youth and old age are often in debate. . . .
She was a fair young wife, her body as slender
As any weasel's, and as soft and tender. . . .
She wore a broad silk **fillet**, rather high,
And certainly she had a **lecherous** eye. . . .   30
The wisest man you met would have to wrench
His fancy to imagine such a wench. . . .
Her mouth was sweet as **mead** or honey—say
A hoard of apples lying in the hay. . . .
Now, gentlemen, this Gallant Nicholas   35
Began to romp about and **make a pass**
At this young woman, happening on her one day,
Her husband being out, down Osney way.
Students are sly, and giving way to whim,
He made a grab and caught her by the limb   40
And said, "O God, I love you! Can't you see
If I don't have you it's the end of me?" . . .
She gave a spring, just like a **skittish** colt
Boxed in a frame for shoeing, and with a jolt
Managed in time to wrench her head away,   45
And said, "Give over, Nicholas, I say!
No, I won't kiss you! Stop it! Let me go
Or I shall scream! I'll let the neighbors know!
Where are your manners? Take away your paws!"
Then Nicholas began to plead his cause   50
And spoke so fair in **proffering** what he could
That in the end she promised him she would,
When she had an opportunity.
"My husband is so full of jealousy,
Unless you watch your step and hold your breath   55
I know for certain it will be my death. . . ."
Said he, "A scholar doesn't have to stir
His wits so much to trick a carpenter."
. . . There was a parish clerk
Serving the church, whose name was Absalon.   60
His hair was all in golden curls and shone;
Just like a fan it strutted outwards, starting
To left and right from an accomplished parting.
Ruddy his face, his eyes as grey as goose,
His shoes cut out in **tracery**, as in use   65
In old St. Paul's. The **hose** upon his feet

Showed scarlet through, and all his clothes were neat
And proper. In a jacket of light blue,
Flounced at the waist and tagged with laces too. . . .
There was no public-house in town or bar   70
He didn't visit with his merry face
If there were **saucy** barmaids round the place.
He was a little **squeamish** in the matter
Of **farting**, and satirical in chatter.
This Absalon, so jolly in his ways,   75
Would bear the censer round on holy days
And **cense** the parish women. He would cast
Many a love-lorn look before he passed,
Especially at this carpenter's young wife;
Looking at her would make a happy life,   80
He thought, so neat, so sweet, so lecherous.
And I daresay if she had been a mouse
And he a cat, she'd have been pounced upon. . . .
What was the good? Were he as bold as brass,
She was in love with gallant Nicholas;   85
However Absalon might blow his horn
His labor won him nothing but her scorn. . . .
Now, show your paces, Nicholas you Spark!
And leave lamenting to the parish clerk.
. . . Nicholas and Alison   90
Agreed at last in what was to be done.
Nicholas was to exercise his wits
On her suspicious husband's foolish fits,
And, if so be the trick worked out all right,
She then would sleep with Nicholas all night. . . .   95
"Now, John," said Nicholas, "believe you me,
I have found out by my astrology,
And looking at the moon when it was bright,
That Monday next, a quarter way through night,
Rain is to fall in torrents, such a **scud**   100
It will be twice as bad as Noah's Flood.
This world," he said, "in just about an hour,
Shall be all drowned, it's such a hideous shower,
And all mankind, with total loss of life."
The carpenter exclaimed, "Alas, my wife! . . .   105
Is there no remedy," he said, "for this?"
"Thanks be to God," said Nicholas, "there is,
If you will do exactly what I say

And don't start thinking up some other way. . . .
I want you, now, at once, to hurry off   110
And fetch a shallow tub or **kneading-trough**
For each of us, but see that they are large
And such as we can float in, like a barge.
And have them loaded with sufficient **victual**
To last a day—we only need a little. . . .   115
And I shall save your wife, you needn't doubt it,
Now off you go, and hurry up about it.
And when the tubs have been collected, three,
That's one for her and for yourself and me,
Then hang them in the roof below the **thatching**   120
That no one may discover what we're **hatching**.
When you have finished doing what I said
And stowed the victuals in them overhead,
Also, an axe to **hack** the ropes apart
So, when the water rises, we can start. . . .   125
Your wife and you must hang some way apart,
For there must be no sin before we start,
No more in longing looks than in the deed.
Those are your orders. Off with you! God speed!" . . .
And on the Monday when it drew to night   130
[John] shut his door and doused the candle-light
And made quite sure all was as it should be.
And shortly, up they **clambered**, all the three. . . .
The carpenter, with all the work he'd seen,
Fell dead asleep—round curfew, must have been . . .   135
And snored because his head was turned **awry**.
Down by their ladders, stalking from on high
Came Nicholas and Alison, and sped
Softly downstairs, without a word, to bed. . . .
And thus lay Nicholas and Alison   140
At busy play in eager quest of fun. . . .
The first cock crew at last, and thereupon
Up rode this jolly lover Absalon . . .
And by the casement window took his stand
Breast-high it stood, no higher than his hand.   145
He gave a cough, no more than half a sound;
"Alison, honeycomb, are you around?" . . .
"You go away," she answered, "you Tom-fool!
There's no come-up-and-kiss-me here for you.
I love another and why shouldn't I too?   150

I want to get some sleep. You go to Hell!"
"Alas!" said Absalon. "I knew it well;
True love is always mocked and girded at;
So kiss me, if you can't do more than that,
For Jesu's love and for the love of me!"   155
"And if I do, will you be off?" said she.
"Promise you darling," answered Absalon.
"Get ready then; wait, I'll put something on. . . ."
She flung the window open then in haste
And said, "Have done, come on, no time to waste,   160
The neighbors here are always on the spy."
Absalon started wiping his mouth dry.
Dark was the night as pitch, as black as coal,
And at the window out she put her hole
And Absalon, so fortune framed the farce,   165
Put up his mouth and kissed her naked **arse**
Most savorously before he knew of this.
And back he started. Something was amiss;
He knew quite well a woman has no beard,
Yet something quite rough and hairy had appeared.   170
"What have I done?" he said. "Can that be you?"
"Teehee!" she cried and **clapped** the window to.
Off went poor Absalon sadly through the dark.
"A beard! a beard!" cried Nicholas the Spark.
Who's busy rubbing, scraping at his lips   175
With dust, with sand, with straw, with cloth, with chips
But Absalon? He thought, "I'll bring him down!
I wouldn't let this go for all the town.
I'd take my soul and sell it to the Devil
To be revenged upon him! I'll get level. . . ."   180
So, weeping like a child that has been whipped,
He turned away; across the road he slipped
And called on Gervase. Gervase was a **smith**;
His forge was full of things for ploughing with. . . .
[Absalon] caught a [poker] up—the haft was cool—   185
And left the **smithy** softly with the tool,
Crept to the little window in the wall
And coughed. He knocked and gave a little call
Under the window as he had before.
Alison said, "There's someone at the door.   190
Who's knocking there? I'll warrant it's a thief."
"Why, no," said he, "my little flower-leaf,

It's your own Absalon, my sweety-thing!
Look what I've brought you—it's a golden ring. . . .
I'll give it to you, darling, for a kiss."   195
Now Nicholas had risen for a piss,
And thought he could improve upon the **jape**
And make him kiss his arse **ere** he escape,
And opening the window with a jerk,
Stuck out his arse, a handsome piece of work,   200
Buttocks and all, as far as to the **haunch**.
Said Absalon, all set to make a launch,
"Speak, pretty bird, I know not where thou art!"
This Nicholas at once let fly a **fart**
As loud as if it were a thunder-clap.   205
He was near blinded by the blast, poor chap,
But his hot iron was ready; with a thump
He [struck] him in the middle of the rump. . . .
"Help! Water! Water! Help! For Heaven's love!"
The carpenter, startled from sleep above,   210
And hearing shouts for water and a thud,
Thought, "Heaven help us! Here come's Nowel's Flood!"
And up he sat and with no more ado
He took his axe and [cut] the ropes in two
And down went everything. He didn't stop   215
To sell his bread and ale, but came down flop
Upon the floor and fainted right away.
Up started Alison and Nicholay
And shouted, "Help!" and "Murder!" in the street.
The neighbors all came running up in heat. . . .   220
[John's] arm in falling had been broken double.
But still he was obliged to face his trouble,
For when he spoke he was at once borne down
By Nicholas and his wife. They told the town
That he was mad, there'd got into his blood   225
Some sort of nonsense about "Nowel's Flood,"
That vain imaginings and fantasy
Had made him buy the kneading-tubs, that he
Had hung them in the rafter up above
And that he'd begged them both for heaven's love   230
To sit up in the roof for company.
All started laughing at this lunacy
And streamed upstairs to **gape** and pry and poke,
And treated all his sufferings as a joke.

No matter what the carpenter asserted   235
It went for nothing, no one was converted;
With powerful oaths they swore the fellow down
And he was held mad by all the town;
Even the learned said to one another,
"The fellow must be crazy, my dear brother."   240
So to a general laughter he succumbed.
That's how the carpenter's young wife was **plumbed**
For all the tricks his jealousy could try,
And Absalon has kissed her **nether** eye
And Nicholas is branded on the **bum**.   245
And God bring all of us to Kingdom Come.

Vocabulary

*arse *(n.)*   ass; buttocks (often considered vulgar)
*astrolabe *(n.)*   medieval instrument used to calculate the position of
    heavenly bodies
awry *(adv.)*   in a turned or twisted position
*bum *(n.)*   (chiefly British) buttocks (sometimes considered vulgar)
*cense *(v.)*   to perfume with a covered incense burner
clamber *(v.)*   to climb awkwardly; to scramble
clap *(v.)*   to slam
*codger *(n.)*   affectionate or mildly derogatory term for an old man
*ere *(conj.)*   before
fart (farting) *(n.)*   expulsion of intestinal gas (usually considered vulgar)
*fillet *(n.)*   ribbon or narrow strip of material used especially as a head-
    band
*flounced *(adj.)*   trimmed with a wide ruffle
*gallant *(adj.)*   courteously and elaborately attentive, especially to ladies
gape *(v.)*   to look at stupidly or in open-mouthed surprise or wonder
*geomancy *(n.)*   practice of foretelling future events or discovering hid-
    den knowledge by means of figures, lines, or geographic features
hack *(v.)*   to chop
hatch *(v.)*   to plan in secret
*haunch *(n.)*   hip
hose *(n.)*   stockings
*jape *(n.)*   joke
*kip *(n.)*   sleeping place
*kneading-trough/tub *(n.)*   container for making bread dough

*Denotes low-frequency word.

lecherous *(adj.)*   given to indulgence or sexual activity
lodger *(n.)*   roomer
make a pass *(v.)*   to make a sexually inviting gesture
***mead** *(n.)*   fermented beverage made of water, honey, malt, and yeast
nether *(adj.)*   situated under or below
***plumb** *(v.)*   to probe the depths of
proffer *(v.)*   to present for acceptance
saucy *(adj.)*   bold and impudent
***scud** *(n.)*   rain driven by wind
skittish *(adj.)*   nervous
smith *(n.)*   worker in metals
***smithy** *(n.)*   metal workshop
squeamish *(adj.)*   easily nauseated or disgusted
sting (stung) *(v.)*   to cheat
***thatching** *(n.)*   plant material, such as straw, used as a roof for a house
***tracery** *(n.)*   decorative openwork
***victuals** *(n.)*   food

Activities

1. As a class, read lines 60 through 88, which describe Absalon. What specific details about Absalon does Chaucer use to develop his character? What is your impression of him? How does Chaucer prepare us for what happens to Absalon?

2. With your study group, choose a second character from "The Miller's Tale." What is this character like? How does Chaucer's description of this character relate to what happens later in the tale? Record your ideas in your journal.

3. After 600 years, why do we still laugh at "The Miller's Tale"? What is the serious side or moral in this story? What makes this tale a satire of medieval society and literary conventions? Make notes in your journal, using details from the story to support your ideas.

4. Write an essay on Chaucer's satire of medieval society.

5. Working alone or with your study group, write a short tale set in medieval times, using some of Chaucer's techniques, such as physically describing the characters, using humor, and teaching a moral lesson. You may want to use one of the following as a main character for your story: sailor, nun, student, lawyer, or physician.

6. If you have read "Bisclavret," write an essay comparing Absalon and Bisclavret as courtly lovers. What is the situation of each one at the end of his story?

*Denotes low-frequency word.

For Further Reading

Brewer, Derek, ed. *Chaucer: The Critical Heritage.* 2 vols. London: Routledge, 1978.

Chaucer, Geoffrey. *The Canterbury Tales.* Trans. Nevill Coghill. 1952. Baltimore: Penguin, 1975.

Coghill, Nevill. *The Poet Chaucer.* 2nd ed. New York: Oxford UP, 1968.

Howard, Donald R. *Chaucer: His Life, His Works, His World.* New York: Dutton, 1987.

CHAPTER 8

From *Romeo and Juliet*

William Shakespeare (1564–1616)
Drama: Tragedy

Background

As the prolific author of poetry, history plays, tragedies, and come-dies, Shakespeare continues to be regarded as one of the greatest writers in the English language. Most of his life was spent under the reign of Elizabeth I, a time when drama in England flourished. Shakespeare's ca-reer was unusual in that he managed his own London theater company, wrote the plays that the company performed, and acted in them as well. Moreover, he was an owner of two theaters, the Globe and the Blackfriars.

Romeo and Juliet is one of the greatest love tragedies of all time. The story of tragic young lovers was a popular one in the plays and novels of the Renaissance. Shakespeare's direct source for the play appears to have been a poem in English, "The Tragical History of Romeus and Juliet," writ-ten by Arthur Brooke in 1562. Shakespeare adapts Brooke freely, and his skill as a dramatist can be seen in the play resulting from the adaptation.

An inspiration for later musical compositions, ballets, and other artistic interpretations, Romeo and Juliet are probably the world's most fa-mous pair of star-crossed lovers.

Pre-Reading Activities

1. With your class, discuss the differences between traditional and mod-ern ways of contracting a marriage.
2. In your journal, make a list of reasons why, in your opinion, some

families cannot get along with other families. Then discuss your ideas
with your small group or class.

Key Terms

blood feud   heir/heiress
courtly love   London
Elizabeth I (1533–1603)   Renaissance
Elizabethan England   Shakespearean sonnet
empire   Stratford-on-Avon
Fate (the Stars)   "The Tragical History of Romeus and
Globe Theater   Juliet" (Arthur Brooke, 1562)

From *Romeo and Juliet*
William Shakespeare

Characters for These Scenes

CHORUS
JULIET, a daughter of the Capulet family
ROMEO, a son of the Montague family

Prologue

[*Enter*] CHORUS: Two households, both alike in dignity,
   In fair **Verona**, where we lay our scene,
   From ancient grudge break new **mutiny**,
   Where **civil** blood makes **civil** hands unclean.
   From forth the fatal **loins** of these two **foes**   5
   A pair of **star-crossed** lovers take their life;
   Whose misadventured **piteous overthrows**
   Doth with their death bury their parents' strife.
   The fearful passage of their death-marked love,
   And the continuance of their parents' rage,   10
   Which, but their children's end, **nought** could remove,
   Is now the two hours' **traffic** of our stage;
   The which if you with patient ears attend,
   What here shall miss, our **toil** shall strive to **mend**.
[*Exit*]

Figure 13 • Balcony scene from *Romeo and Juliet*, as portrayed in the film by director Franco Zeffirelli *(Everett Collection)*

Act II, Scene II

[*Romeo advances*]

ROMEO: He **jests** at scars that never felt a wound.

[*Enter Juliet above at her window*]

But soft, what light through yonder window breaks?
It is the east, and Juliet is the sun.
Arise, fair sun, and kill the envious moon,
Who is already sick and pale with grief   5
That thou, her maid, art far more fair than she.
Be not her maid, since she is **envious**;
Her **vestal livery** is but **sick and green**,
And none but fools do wear it; **cast it off**.
It is my lady, O, it is my love!   10
O that she knew she were!
She speaks, yet she says nothing; what of that?

Her eye **discourses**, I will answer it.
I am too bold, 'tis not to me she speaks.
Two of the fairest stars in all the heaven,   15
Having some business, [do] entreat her eyes
To twinkle in their spheres till they return.
What if her eyes were there, they in her head?
The brightness of her cheek would shame those stars,
As daylight doth a lamp; her [eyes] in heaven   20
Would through the airy region stream so bright
That birds would sing and think it were not night.
See how she leans her cheek upon her hand!
O that I were a glove upon that hand,
That I might touch that cheek!   25

JULIET: Ay me!

ROMEO: She speaks!
    O, speak again, bright angel, for thou art
As glorious to this night, being o'er my head,
As is a winged messenger of heaven
Unto the white-upturned wond'ring eyes
Of mortals that fall back to gaze on him,   30
When he **bestrides** the lazy puffing clouds,
And sails upon the bosom of the air.

JULIET: O Romeo, Romeo, wherefore art thou Romeo?
    Deny thy father and refuse thy name;
    Or, if thou wilt not, be but sworn by my love,   35
    And I'll no longer be a Capulet.

ROMEO [*Aside*]: Shall I hear more, or shall I speak at this?

JULIET: 'Tis but thy name that is my enemy;
    Thou art thyself, though not a Montague.
    What's Montague? It is nor hand nor foot,   40
    Nor arm nor face, [nor any other part]
    Belonging to a man. O, be some other name!
    What's in a name? That which we call a rose
    By any other word would smell as sweet;
    So Romeo would, were he not Romeo called,   45
    Retain that dear perfection which he owes
    Without that title. Romeo, **doff** thy name,
    And for thy name, which is no part of thee,
    Take all myself.

ROMEO: I take thee at thy word.   50

Call me but love, and I'll be new baptized;
Henceforth I never will be Romeo.

JULIET: What man art thou that thus **bescreened** in night
So stumblest on my **counsel**?

ROMEO: By a name
I know not how to tell thee who I am.   55
My name, dear saint, is hateful to myself,
Because it is an enemy to thee;
Had I it written, I would tear the word.

JULIET: My ears have yet not drunk a hundred words
Of thy tongue's uttering, yet I know the sound.   60
Art thou not Romeo, and a Montague?

ROMEO: Neither, fair maid, if either thee dislike.

JULIET: How camest thou **hither**, tell me and wherefore?
The orchard walls are high and hard to climb,
And the place death, considering who thou art,   65
If any of my kinsmen find thee here.

ROMEO: With love's light wings did I **o'erperch** these walls.
For stony limits cannot hold love out.
And what love can do, that dares love attempt;
Therefore thy kinsmen are no stop to me.   70

JULIET: If they do see thee, they will **murther** thee.

ROMEO: Alack, there lies more peril in thine eye
Than twenty of their swords! Look thou but sweet,
And I am **proof** against their **enmity**.

JULIET: I would not for the world they saw thee here.   75

ROMEO: I have night's **cloak** to hide me from their eyes,
And but thou love me, let them find me here;
My life were better ended by their hate,
Than death [put off], wanting of thy love.

JULIET: By whose direction foundest thou out this place?   80

ROMEO: By love, that first did prompt me to inquire;
He lent me counsel, and I lent him eyes.
I am no pilot, yet wert thou as far
As that vast shore [washed] with the farthest sea,
I should adventure for such merchandise.   85

JULIET: Thou knowest the mask of night is on my face,
Else would a maiden **blush bepaint** my cheek
For that which thou hast heard me speak to-night.

Fain would I dwell on form, fain, fain, deny
What I have spoke, but farewell **compliment**!   90
Dost thou love me? I know thou wilt say, "Ay,"
And I will take thy word; yet, if thou swearest,
Thou mayest prove false: at lovers' **perjuries**
They say **Jove** laughs. O gentle Romeo,
If thou dost love, pronounce it faithfully;   95
Or if thou thinkest I am too quickly won,
I'll frown and be perverse, and say thee **nay**,
So thou wilt woo, but else not for the world.
In truth, fair Montague, I am too fond,
And therefore thou mayest think my behavior light,   100
But trust me, gentleman, I'll prove more true
Than those that have [more] **coying** to be **strange**.
I should have been more strange, I must confess,
But that thou overheardst, ere I was ware,
My true-love passion; therefore pardon me,   105
And not **impute** this yielding to light love,
Which the dark night hath so discovered.

ROMEO: Lady, by yonder blessed moon I vow,
  That tips with silver all these fruit-tree tops—

JULIET: O, swear not by the moon, the inconstant moon,   110
  That monthly changes in her [circled] orb,
  Lest that thy love prove likewise variable.

ROMEO: What shall I swear by?

JULIET: Do not swear at all;
  Or if thy wilt, swear by thy gracious self,
  Which is the god of my **idolatry**,   115
  And I'll believe thee.

ROMEO: If my heart's dear love—

JULIET: Well, do not swear. Although I joy in thee,
  I have no joy of this contract to-night,
  It is too rash, too unadvised, too sudden,
  Too like the lightning, which doth cease to be   120
  Ere one can say it lightens. Sweet, good night!
  This bud of love, by summer's ripening breath,
  May prove a beauteous flower when next we meet.
  Good night, good night! as sweet repose and rest
  Come to thy heart as that within my breast!   125

ROMEO: O, wilt thou leave me so unsatisfied?

JULIET: What satisfaction canst thou have to-night?

ROMEO: The exchange of thy love's faithful vow for mine.

JULIET: I gave thee mine before thou didst request it;
    And yet I would it were to give again.   130

ROMEO: Wouldst thou withdraw it? for what purpose, love?

JULIET: But to be frank and give it thee again,
    And yet I wish for but the thing I have.
    My **bounty** is as boundless as the sea,
    My love as deep; the more I give to thee,   135
    The more I have, for both are infinite.

[*Nurse calls within*]

    I hear some noise within; dear love, adieu!
    Anon, good nurse! Sweet Montague, be true.
    Stay but a little, I will come again.

[*Exit above*]

ROMEO: O blessed, blessed night! I am afeard,   140
    Being in night, all this is but a dream,
    Too flattering-sweet to be substantial.

[*Enter Juliet above*]

JULIET: Three words, dear Romeo, and good night indeed.
    If that thy **bent of love** be honorable,
    Thy purpose marriage, send me word tomorrow,   145
    By one that I'll procure to come to thee,
    Where and what time thou wilt perform the rite,
    And all my fortunes at thy foot I'll lay,
    And follow thee my lord throughout the world.

NURSE [*Within*]: Madam!   150

JULIET: I come, anon.—But, if thou meanest not well,
    I do **beseech** thee—

NURSE [*Within*]: Madam!

JULIET: **By and by**, I come—
    To cease thy strife, and leave me to my grief.
    To-morrow will I send.

ROMEO: So **thrive** my soul—

JULIET: A thousand times good night! [*Exit above*]   155

ROMEO: A thousand times the worse, to want thy light.
    Love goes toward love as schoolboys from their books,
    But love from love, toward school with heavy looks.

[*Retiring*]

Vocabulary

PROLOGUE

civil *(adj.)*   relating to citizens; civilized
foe *(n.)*   enemy
***loins** *(n. pl.)*   reproductive organs
mend *(v.)*   to correct; to set right
***mutiny** *(n.)*   bitter conflict
***nought** (also **naught**) *(n.)*   nothing
***overthrow** *(n.)*   upset
piteous *(adj.)*   arousing pity or compassion
***star-crossed** *(adj.)*   not favored by the stars; ill-fated
toil *(n.)*   labor; effort
***traffic** *(n.)*   business; dealings
***Verona** *(n.)*   city in northeastern Italy

ACT II, SCENE II

***anon** *(adv.)*   presently; soon
***bent of love** *(n.)*   love's intent or resolve
***bepaint** *(v.)*   to color; to tinge
***bescreened** *(adj.)*   screened; covered
***beseech** *(v.)*   to beg for urgently or earnestly
***bestride** *(v.)*   to walk across
blush *(n.)*   reddening of the face
bounty *(n.)*   generosity
***by and by** *(adv.)*   before long; soon
cast [something] off *(v.)*   to remove [something]
***cloak** *(n.)*   loose outer garment
***compliment** *(n.)*   social courtesy
***counsel** *(n.)*   guarded thoughts
***coying** *(n.)*   cute or coquettish playfulness
***discourse** *(v.)*   to talk
***doff** *(v.)*   to remove; to put aside
enmity *(n.)*   hatred; hostility
envious *(adj.)*   feeling or showing envy (the desire to possess something
  belonging to another)
***fain** *(adv.)*   with pleasure
***hither** *(adv.)*   here
idolatry *(n.)*   excessive devotion to a person or thing
***impute** *(v.)*   to charge; to attribute
jest *(v.)*   to make fun of; to mock
***Jove (Jupiter)** *(prop. n.)*   chief Roman god

*Denotes low-frequency word.

*lest *(conj.)* for fear
*livery *(n.)* clothing; garb
*murther *(n.)* old form of *murder*
*nay *(n.)* no
*o'erperch *(v.)* to go over and rest on, as on a bird's perch or roost
perjury *(n.)* false swearing
*proof *(adj.)* able to resist
*sick and green *(adj. phrase)* suffering a kind of anemia thought in
    Shakespeare's time to be found in single girls
*strange *(adj.)* distant; external
thrive *(v.)* to be successful; to flourish
*vestal *(adj.)* pure; virginal

Activities

1. Read the Prologue closely. What is its function? Make notes in your journal and discuss your ideas with your class.
2. If you have read *Antigone*, compare its Prologue to that of *Romeo and Juliet*.
3. Read the dialogue aloud, with the entire class reading the chorus, male students reading Romeo's lines, and female students reading Juliet's lines.
4. Romeo and Juliet decide to marry against their parents' wishes. Do you agree or disagree with their decision? Justify your answer.
5. Alone or with a partner, write a dialogue in modern English between a young man and woman who are in love but do not have their parents' approval to marry. Have your characters decide what they are going to do about their situation.
6. Write an essay arguing for or against young people's marrying against their parents' wishes.
7. If you have read "Bisclavret," write an essay on Romeo and Juliet as courtly lovers.

For Further Reading

Burgess, Anthony. *Shakespeare*. New York: Knopf, 1970.
Cahn, Victor L. *Shakespeare the Playwright*. New York: Greenwood, 1991.
Shakespeare, William. *The Riverside Shakespeare*. Ed. G. Blakemore Evans. Boston: Houghton, 1974.

Additional Reading

Sonnet 29

William Shakespeare
Oral Tradition and Poetry: Sonnet

> When, in disgrace with Fortune and men's eyes,
> I all alone beweep my outcast state,
> And trouble deaf heaven with my bootless cries,
> And look upon myself and curse my fate,
> Wishing me like to one more rich in hope,   5
> Featured like him, like him with friends possessed,
> Desiring this man's art and that man's scope,
> With what I most enjoy contented least;
> Yet in these thoughts myself almost despising
> Haply I think on thee, and then my state,   10
> Like to the lark at break of day arising
> From sullen earth, sings hymns at heaven's gate:
> For thy sweet love remember'd such wealth brings
> That then I scorn to change my state with kings.

Activities

1. What is the state of mind of the speaker at the beginning of the sonnet? In which lines do his feelings change? Why do they change?
2. Compare the poet's attitude toward love in Sonnet 29 with his attitude in *Romeo and Juliet*.
3. Write an essay on love in Shakespeare's tragedy *Romeo and Juliet* and in Sonnet 29.

For Further Reading

Rougemont, Denis de. *Love in the Western World*. New York: Harper, 1974.

9

Romantic Poetry

Johann Friedrich von Schiller (1759–1805) and William Wordsworth (1770–1850)

Oral Tradition and Poetry: Ode and Sonnet

Key Terms

Beethoven, Ludwig van
  (1770–1827)
Enlightenment
individualism
metonymy
pathetic fallacy

personification
rational
Romanticism
Symphony No. 9, opus 125
  (by Beethoven)
universal brotherhood

Pre-Reading Activities

1. How do you think an artist, especially a poet, might react to a period in which reason and scientific thinking prevail?
2. Listen to the last movement of Beethoven's Ninth Symphony. Record your thoughts and feelings as you listen.
3. How are poetry and music related?

Background: Schiller

During Schiller's lifetime, Germany was a center of great intellectual activity in many fields. Important German trends are reflected in

Schiller's life as well as in his philosophical and literary works. Together, they embodied and helped to define major preoccupations of European culture in the Romantic period, which reached from the end of the eighteenth through much of the nineteenth century.

Living in a period of violent political upheaval that resulted in the overthrow of absolute monarchies, Schiller was concerned with supranational issues such as universal brotherhood, freedom, and humane government. He is best known as the author of dramatic tragedies such as *Mary Stuart* and *Don Carlos* (1787). Much of Schiller's literary work became the basis for musical interpretations, including operas. His poem "Ode to Joy" was set to music by Beethoven in his Ninth Symphony in 1824.

From "Ode to Joy"
Johann Friedrich von Schiller

Joy, thou source of heaven-sent light,
Daughter of **Elysium**.
    Touched with fire, to the site
Of thy shining shrine we come.
    What Custom's strength divides from others   5
Thy pure magic union brings;
    Men throughout the world are brothers
In safety of thy wings.

    Millions, turn and come together!
Share this universal kiss!   10
Brothers—over a heavenly **bliss**
    Must reign our all-loving Father.

    He who for achievement may long,
Of strong friendship may be sure,
    He who has a wife to treasure,   15
Let him join our mighty song.
    Yes—If exists a single being
Who on earth calls one heart his own,
    And denies it—then, unseeing,
Let him go and weep alone.   20

    Joy is drunk by all the creatures
From the Earth's abundant breast;
    All things good and bad are Nature's,

And with blameless joy are blessed.
    Joy to us gives love and wine,   25
Friendship that will last 'til death;
    The lowly worm feels life divine,
As the angel near God's breast.

    Glad, as when the suns run glorious
Through the Heaven's dazzling skies,   30
Brothers, run with shining eyes
    Heroes, happy and victorious.

    Millions, turn and come together!
Share this universal kiss!
Brothers, over a heavenly bliss   35
    Must reign our all-loving Father.

    Do the millions, His creation,
Know Him and His works of love?
Find Him in the heights above.
    Brothers! Brothers!   40
    In the heights above
Is His starry **habitation**!

    Joy, O daughter of Elysium,
Thy pure magic union brings;
What Custom's strength divides from others   45
    Men throughout the world are brothers
In the safety of thy wings.
Joy, thou source of heaven-sent light,
Daughter of Elysium.

Vocabulary

bliss *(n.)*   spiritual joy
***Elysium** *(n.)*   in Greek mythology, the place of ideal happiness; paradise
habitation *(n.)*   home

Background: Wordsworth

    Outstanding among the great English Romantic poets, Wordsworth is well known for his poetic collections *Lyrical Ballads* and *The Prelude*,

*Denotes low-frequency word.

which he continued reworking until his death. Like most of his poems, the ballads are autobiographical. With deeply personal detail, Wordsworth records in recollection his travels in England and on the European continent in the company of his sister Dorothy; together they encounter the wonders and permanence of nature and contemplate the brief, hard lives of human beings.

Wordsworth sympathized with the struggle for the common man to be free, and, at the beginning of the French Revolution in 1789, looked with favor on the overthrow of the monarchy. After the violence of the French mob got out of hand, however, he became more conservative. Still, these poems represent his enthusiasm for freedom and brotherhood as well as his love of nature. The years given for each poem are dates of publication. The date on the left is the first year the poem was published, and the date on the right is the year this version was published. The first poem is a sonnet.

"To Toussaint L'Ouverture"
William Wordsworth

Toussaint, the most unhappy man of men!
Whether the whistling Rustic tend his plough
Within thy hearing, or thy head be now

Figure 14 • *Summer Afternoon, Arundel Castle,* **by the Romantic painter George Cole (British, 1810–83)** *(©Sotheby Parke-Bernet)*

Pillowed in some deep **dungeon's earless den**:—
O miserable **Chieftain**! where and when   5
Wilt thou find patience? Yet die not; do thou
Wear rather in thy bonds a cheerful brow:
Though fallen thyself, never to rise again,
Live, and take comfort. Thou hast left behind
Powers that will work for thee; air, earth, and skies;   10
There's not a breathing of the common wind
That will forget thee; thou hast great allies;
Thy friends are exultations, agonies,
And love, and man's unconquerable mind.   14

1802   1803

"My Heart Leaps Up When I Behold"
William Wordsworth

My heart leaps up when I behold
    A rainbow in the sky;
So was it when my life began;
So is it now I am a man;
So be it when I shall grow old,   5
    Or let me die!
The child is father of the Man;
And I could wish my days to be
Bound each to each by natural **piety**.

1802   1807

"The World Is Too Much
with Us; Late and Soon"
William Wordsworth

The world is too much with us; late and soon,
Getting and spending, we lay waste our powers:
Little we see in Nature that is ours;
We have given our hearts away, a **sordid boon**!
This Sea that bares her bosom to the moon;   5
The winds that will be howling at all hours,
And are up-gathered now like sleeping flowers;
For this, for everything, we are out of tune;

It moves us not.—Great God! I'd rather be
A **Pagan suckled** in a **creed** outworn;   10
So might I, standing on this pleasant **lea**,
Have glimpses that would make me less forlorn;
Have sight of **Proteus** rising from the sea;
Or hear old **Triton** blow his **wreathed** horn.

1802–1804   1807

Vocabulary

"To Toussaint L'Ouverture"

*chieftain *(n.)*   leader of a group, usually a clan or tribe
den *(n.)*   cave
dungeon *(n.)*   prison
*earless *(adj.)*   without ears; here, a metonym to indicate that no
   human being is present to hear
L'Ouverture, Toussaint (1743–1803) *(prop. n.)*   Haitian general,
   liberator, and governor of Haiti from 1801 to 1802

"My Heart Leaps Up When I Behold"

piety *(n.)*   devotion and reverence

"The World Is Too Much with Us; Late and Soon"

*boon *(n.)*   favor or blessing given to someone
creed *(n.)*   formal statement of religious belief
*lea *(n.)*   grassland; meadow
pagan *(n.)*   any non-Christian
*Proteus *(prop. n.)*   in Greek mythology, a sea god who could
   change his shape
sordid *(adj.)*   dirty; morally degraded
suckled *(adj.)*   nursed or brought up, as a child
*Triton *(prop. n.)*   in Greek mythology, a sea god having a man's head
   and a fish's tail
wreathed *(adj.)*   in a circle or spiral, like a conch shell

Activities

1.   Read each poem aloud. What feelings are being conveyed by the poet?
     What images does he use to accomplish this? What is the rhyme
     scheme of the poem?

*Denotes low-frequency word.

2. A common theme of the Romantic poets is freedom. Select one poem, read it carefully, and note in your journal the images used by the poet to express his feelings and thoughts about freedom.

3. Write an essay on nature or brotherhood in the poetry of Schiller and Wordsworth. If you cite lines from the poetry, use quotation marks (". . .") around the quoted material and give the line number in parentheses. For example:

    Wordsworth believes that Toussaint L'Ouverture does not suffer alone, for he is accompanied by "exultations, agonies, / And love. . ." (13–14).

4. Write an essay comparing Romantic poetry and music.

For Future Reading

Johnson, Paul. *The Birth of the Modern: World Society 1815–1830*. New York: Harper, 1991.

Mahoney, John L. *The English Romantics: Major Poetry and Critical Theory.* Lexington, MA: Heath, 1978.

Ungar, Frederick. *Friedrich Schiller: An Anthology for Our Time*. New York: Ungar, 1959.

CHAPTER 10

"Ain't I a Woman?"

Sojourner Truth (ca. 1797–1883)
Nonfiction: Autobiographical Essay

Background

An African-American born into slavery in New York State as Isabella Van Wagener, Sojourner Truth fled to freedom in 1827 and renamed herself after experiencing religious visions. In 1850, she began her courageous tours of the United States, speaking out for the abolition of slavery. An eloquent speaker, Sojourner Truth drew large crowds. Although she was illiterate most of her life, she dictated her autobiography, *The Narrative of Sojourner Truth* (1850), sales of which helped to earn her living. She later supported an independent state for freed slaves and joined the women's suffrage movement; spirituality continued to be one of her major concerns.

"Ain't I a Woman?" is the title given to a speech made by Sojourner Truth at the second annual Women's Rights Convention, which was held in Akron, Ohio, in 1852, when she was over 50 years old. Men and women gathered at this convention to discuss whether women should have the same political and social rights as men. After formal speeches, anyone who wished to get up and speak could do so. Most of the speakers were men, because during the nineteenth century it was considered improper for a woman to speak in public.

On the second day of the convention, several clergymen spoke against women's rights. All of them gave reasons why the status of women should be lower than that of men. For example, one minister said that women deserved lower status than men because of the sin committed by Eve in the Garden of Eden. After these men had spoken, Sojourner Truth rose and moved to the front of the room. "Ain't I a Woman?" is her reply to their speeches.

Pre-Reading Activities

1. With your study group or class, discuss the meaning of democracy. Should all citizens be treated alike?
2. With your study group or class, discuss the ways in which human rights can be extended to include groups that did not have them before.

Key Terms

abolition   feminist movement
African-American   Liberia
American Civil War (1861–1865)   Underground Railroad
emancipation   women's suffrage movement

"Ain't I a Woman?"
Sojourner Truth

Well, children, where there is so much **racket** there must   1
be something out of **kilter**. I think that 'twixt the negroes of the
South and the women at the North, all talking about rights, the
white men will be in a **fix** pretty soon. But what's all this here talking about?

That man over there says that women need to be helped into   2
carriages, and lifted over **ditches**, and to have the best place everywhere. Nobody ever helps me into carriages, or over mud-puddles, or
gives me any best place! And **ain't** I a woman? Look at me! Look at
my arm! I have **plowed** and planted, and gathered into barns, and
no man could **head** me! And ain't I a woman? I could work as much
and eat as much as a man—when I could get it—and **bear** the **lash**
as well! And ain't I a woman? I have **borne** thirteen children, and
seen them most all sold off to slavery, and when I cried out with my
mother's grief, none but Jesus heard me! And ain't I a woman?

Figure 15 • Sojourner Truth (d. 1883) *(Sophia Smith Collection, Smith College)*

Then they talk about this thing in the head; what's this they   3
call it? [Intellect, someone whispers.] That's it, honey. What's that
got to do with women's rights or negroes' rights? If my cup won't
hold but a pint, and yours holds a quart, wouldn't you be **mean** not
to let me have my little half-measure full?

Then that little man in black there, he says women can't have   4
as much rights as men, 'cause Christ wasn't a woman! Where did
your Christ come from? Where did your Christ come from? From
God and a woman! Man had nothing to do with Him.

If the first woman God ever made was strong enough to turn   5
the world upside down all alone, these women together ought to be
able to turn it back, and get it right side up again! And now they is
asking to do it, the men better let them.

Obliged to you for hearing me, and now old Sojourner ain't   6
got nothing more to say.

Vocabulary

ain't *(v.)*   aren't (nonstandard English)
bear (bore, borne) *(v.)*   to give birth to; to endure
ditch *(n.)*   long, narrow trench dug in the earth, usually for drainage
fix *(n.)*   difficult position
head *(v.)*   to be ahead of; to surpass
*kilter *(n.)*   order
lash *(n.)*   whip
mean *(adj.)*   characterized by petty selfishness or malice
obliged to you *(v. phrase)*   a way to say "thank you"
plow *(v.)*   to work with a plow (an agricultural tool used to prepare the
    earth for planting)
racket *(n.)*   confused, clattering noise; clamor
*'twixt *(prep.)*   between

Activities

1. Read the text closely. Who do you think is the speaker's audience?
    What parts of Sojourner Truth's speech give it an informal tone? What
    aspects make it formal?
2. What are the two arguments Sojourner Truth is making? How does
    she relate the two? How does she organize her thoughts to persuade
    her audience?
3. Notice that Sojourner Truth makes many references to religion in her
    speech. Why do you think she does this? Is it effective?
4. Write a summary of Sojourner Truth's argument for giving women the
    right to vote.
5. Write an essay to persuade an audience that a group of people who do
    not have a right to do something should be allowed to have that right.
    Before writing your essay, be sure to have a clear idea of who your au-
    dience is. This should help you to plan which facts and what tone you
    will use to convince your audience.

For Further Reading

Gilbert, Sandra M., and Susan Gubar, eds. *No Man's Land: The Place of the
    Woman Writer in the Twentieth Century.* Vol. 2: *Sexchanges.* New Haven:
    Yale UP, 1989.

*Denotes low-frequency word.

_____. *The Norton Anthology of Literature by Women: The Tradition in English*. New York: Norton, 1985.

Krass, Peter. *Sojourner Truth*. New York: Chelsea House, 1988.

Loewenberg, Bert James, and Ruth Bogin, eds. *Black Women in Nineteenth-Century American Life*. University Park: Pennsylvania State UP, 1976.

Rogers, Katherine, ed. *Early American Women Writers: From Anne Bradstreet to Louisa May Alcott, 1650–1865*. New York: Meridian, 1991.

11

From *Oliver Twist*

Charles Dickens (1812–1870)
Fiction: Novel

Background

The year of Charles Dickens's birth saw his native England engaged in war against Napoleon and against the United States. The cost of these wars was high, not only in human lives but in increased taxes that made life even more difficult for the starving poor. In 1824, Dickens's father went to debtors prison, forcing Charles to leave school and go to work in a factory. Thus, he experienced firsthand the sufferings of the poor. After his father's release from prison, he returned to school. But these events had greatly shocked him, and they influenced his writing and haunted him until his death.

As a young man, Dickens became a journalist who contributed well-received stories and essays to magazines and newspapers. Thereafter he began to write serial installments of what would become three of his major novels: *The Pickwick Papers, Oliver Twist,* and *Nicholas Nickleby.* Other well-known works by Dickens are *David Copperfield* (an autobiographical work), *A Christmas Carol, A Tale of Two Cities, Great Expectations,* and *Hard Times.* The realistic details of these works helped the cause of social reform in England. Even today, Dickens is regarded as one of the greatest English novelists.

Written in 1838, *Oliver Twist* was the second Dickens novel published in installments—that is, one small portion at a time. It is the story of an illegitimate orphan boy born in a workhouse and the trials this poor child suffers in nineteenth-century England. For many of the novel's realistic and detailed descriptions of the period, Dickens drew on events from his own childhood. The novel was relevant to the times as a statement against the New Poor Law, passed three years earlier, which was tearing apart the family life of the poor.

Pre-Reading Activities

1. Discuss with your group what you think might happen to poor children whose parents have died.
2. What happens to the poor in an industrialized nation?

Key Terms

autobiographical
"Boz"
debtors prison
Industrial Revolution
irony
novel

picaresque
New Poor Law
Realism
Victorian England
workhouse

From *Oliver Twist*
Charles Dickens

Although I am not disposed to maintain that the being born   1
in a workhouse is in itself the most fortunate and enviable circumstance that can possibly **befall** a human being, I do mean to say that in this particular instance it was the very best thing for Oliver Twist that could by possibility have occurred. The fact is, that there was considerable difficulty in inducing Oliver to take upon himself the **office of respiration**,—a troublesome practice, but one which custom has **rendered** necessary to our easy existence,—and for some time he lay gasping on a little flock mattress, rather unequally poised between this world and the next, the balance being decidedly in favour of the latter.

Now, if during this brief period, Oliver had been surrounded   2
by careful grandmothers, anxious aunts, experienced nurses, and doctors of **profound** wisdom, he would most inevitably and **indubitably** have been killed in no time. There being nobody by, however, but a **pauper** old woman, who was rendered rather misty by an **unwonted** allowance of beer, and a parish surgeon who did such

matters by contract, Oliver and Nature fought out the point between them.

The result was, that, after a few struggles, Oliver breathed, sneezed, and proceeded to advertise to the inmates of the workhouse the fact of a new burden having been imposed upon the **parish**, by setting up as loud a cry as could reasonably have been expected from a male infant who had not been possessed of that very useful **appendage**, a voice, for a much longer space of time than three minutes and a quarter. 3

As Oliver gave this first proof of the free and proper action of his lungs, the patchwork coverlet which was carelessly flung over the iron bedstead, rustled; the pale face of a young female was raised feebly from the pillow; and a faint voice imperfectly **articulated** the words, 'Let me see the child, and die.' 4

. . . The surgeon deposited it in her arms. She **imprinted** her cold white lips passionately on its forehead, passed her hands over her face, gazed wildly round, **shuddered**, fell back—and died. They **chafed** her breast, hands, and temples; but the blood had frozen for ever. They talked of hope and comfort. They had been strangers too long. 5

"It's all over, Mrs. Thingummy," said the surgeon at last. 6

"Ah, poor dear, so it is!" said the nurse, picking up the cork of a green bottle of drink which had fallen out on the pillow as she stooped to take up the child. "Poor dear!" 7

"You needn't **mind** sending up to me, if the child cries, nurse," said the surgeon, putting on his gloves with great deliberation. "It's very likely it *will* be troublesome. Give it a little **gruel** if it is." He put on his hat, and, pausing by the bedside on his way to the door, added, "She was a good-looking girl, too; where did she come from?" 8

"She was brought here last night," replied the old woman, "by the **overseer's** order. She was found lying in the street;—she had walked some distance, for her shoes were worn to pieces; but where she came from, or where she was going to, nobody knows." 9

The surgeon leant over the body, and raised the left hand. "The old story," he said, shaking his head: "no wedding-ring, I see. Ah! Good night!" 10

The medical gentleman walked away to dinner; and the nurse, having once more applied herself to the green bottle, sat down on a low chair before the fire, and proceeded to dress the infant. 11

What an excellent example of the power of dress young Oliver Twist was! Wrapped in the blanket which had **hitherto** formed his only covering, he might have been the child of a nobleman or a beg- 12 gar;—it would have been hard for the **haughtiest** stranger to have fixed his **station** in society. But now that he was enveloped in the old calico robes, which had grown yellow in the same service, he was badged and ticketed, and fell into his place at once—a parish child—the orphan of a workhouse—the humble half-starved **drudge**—to be **cuffed** and **buffeted** through the world,—despised by all, and pitied by none.

Oliver cried **lustily**. If he could have known that he was an orphan, left to the tender mercies of **churchwardens** and overseers, perhaps he would have cried the louder.   13

For the next eight or ten months, Oliver was the victim of a systematic course of treachery and deception—he was brought up by hand. The hungry and **destitute** situation of the infant orphan was **duly** reported by the workhouse authorities to the parish authorities. The parish authorities inquired with dignity of the workhouse authorities, whether there was no female then **domiciled** in "the house" who was in a situation to **impart** to Oliver Twist the consolation and nourishment of which he stood in need.   14

The workhouse authorities replied with humility that there was not. Upon this, the parish authorities **magnanimously** and humanely resolved, that Oliver should be "farmed," or, in other words, that he should be dispatched to a branch-workhouse some three miles off, where twenty or thirty other juvenile offenders against the poor-laws rolled about the floor all day, without the inconvenience of too much food or too much clothing, under the parental superintendence of an elderly female who received the **culprits** at and for the consideration of a sevenpence-halfpenny per small head per week. Sevenpence-halfpenny's worth per week is a good round diet for a child; a great deal may be got for sevenpence-halfpenny—quite enough to overload its stomach, and make it uncomfortable.   15

The elderly female was a woman of wisdom and experience; she knew what was good for children, and she had a very accurate perception of what was good for herself. So, she **appropriated** the greater part of the weekly **stipend** to her own use, and **consigned** the rising **parochial** generation to even a shorter allowance than was originally provided for them; thereby finding in the lowest depth a deeper still, and proving herself a very great experimental philosopher.   16

Everybody knows the story of another experimental philosopher, who had a great theory about a horse being able to live without eating, and who demonstrated it so well, that he got his own horse down to a straw a day, and would have unquestionably have rendered him a very spirited and **rampacious** animal on nothing at all,   17 if he had not died, just four-and-twenty hours before he was to have had his first comfortable **bait** of air.

Unfortunately for the experimental philosophy of the female to whose protecting care Oliver Twist was delivered over, a similar result usually attended the operation of *her* system; for at the very moment when a child had **contrived** to exist upon the smallest possible portion of the weakest possible food, it did **perversely** happen in eight and a half cases out of ten, either that it sickened from **want** and cold, or fell into the fire from neglect, or got half **smothered** by accident; in any one of which cases, the miserable little being was usually summoned into another world, and there gathered to the fathers it had never known in this.

18

Vocabulary

appendage *(n.)* subordinate part
appropriate *(v.)* to take without authority or right
articulate *(v.)* to utter; to speak
*bait *(n.)* snack, taste
befall *(v.)* to happen to, especially as if by fate
*buffet *(v.)* to drive or move, as if by repeated blows
*chafe *(v.)* to warm by rubbing
*churchwarden *(n.)* church officer responsible for money or goods given to help the poor, and for church property
consign *(v.)* to transfer; to deliver
contrive *(v.)* to manage
*cuff *(v.)* to strike with the palm of the hand
culprit *(n.)* one guilty of a crime or fault
destitute *(adj.)* lacking necessities of life; very poor
*domiciled *(adj.)* provided with a home
*drudge *(n.)* one who is obliged to do unpleasant work
duly *(adv.)* properly
*gruel *(n.)* thin porridge (a soft food made from grains or legumes)
haughtiest *(adj.)* most scornfully proud
*hitherto *(adv.)* up to this time
impart *(v.)* to give or grant, as from a supply
imprint *(v.)* to mark by pressure
indubitably *(adv.)* unquestionably
lustily *(adv.)* vigorously; heartily
magnanimously *(adv.)* nobly and generously
mind *(v.)* to be concerned about; to care

*Denotes low-frequency word.

*office of respiration *(n.)*   breathing
*overseer *(n.)*   supervisor
parish *(n.)*   area committed to one pastor (a Christian religious leader)
parochial *(adj.)*   of or relating to a parish
*pauper *(adj.)*   very poor
perversely *(adv.)*   contrarily
profound *(adj.)*   deep
*rampacious *(adj.)*   not easily controlled
render *(v.)*   to cause to become; to make
shudder *(v.)*   to shake or tremble suddenly and violently
smothered *(adj.)*   overcome or killed from lack of air
station *(n.)*   place; position
stipend *(n.)*   fixed sum of money paid periodically for services or expenses
*unwonted *(adj.)*   unusual; unaccustomed
*want *(n.)*   extreme poverty

Activities

1. How do we know from the first moment that Oliver Twist's life will be difficult?
2. Look closely at the text. Select one or two passages where Dickens uses strong irony—that is, where he says the direct opposite of what he means. What does he *really* mean in the passage?
3. What are the attitudes of the adults in charge of Oliver Twist's care? What tone does Dickens use to describe them?
4. With your study group or class, discuss what you think might happen to Oliver Twist as he grows up. Justify your views.
5. In *Oliver Twist*, Dickens shows negative effects of the Industrial Revolution in England. Write an essay discussing both the positive and the negative sides of industrialization.
6. Based on your notes and class discussion, write an essay on Dickens's use of irony to criticize his contemporary society.

For Further Reading

Ackroyd, Peter. *Dickens.* New York: Harper, 1990.
_____. *An Introduction to Dickens.* New York: Ballantine, 1991.
Mankowitz, Wolf. *Dickens of London.* New York: Macmillan, 1976.

*Denotes low-frequency word.

CHAPTER 12

From *The Turn of the Screw*

Henry James (1843–1916)
Fiction: Novella

Background

Born into a distinguished family of writers from New York, Henry James grew up in close contact with European culture. He attended Harvard University, following his brother William, who later became a famous psychologist. After graduation, James began his career writing literary, theater, and art reviews and essays for monthly magazines. By 1875, he had moved permanently to England. In 1915, distressed by the slowness of the United States to enter World War I, James decided to become a British citizen. A master of the art of fiction, he was a radical experimenter who contributed to shaping the modern novel. His best-known novels are *The Portrait of a Lady* and *Daisy Miller*.

The Turn of the Screw shows a clear Romantic influence. It resembles the nineteenth-century literary form of the Gothic tale, a story combining realism and the supernatural. Such stories contain dark castles, the appearance of supernatural beings such as ghosts, and horrible and frightening events. A struggle between good and evil forces is a common Gothic theme, with one character representing the good and another figure, a double, symbolizing evil. Freudian critics see this threatening evil as disguised urges from a primitive, uncontrolled ego and generally trace these urges to the nineteenth-century repression of sexual feelings.

The main framed story of *The Turn of the Screw* is told by the governess, and we do not know whether or not she is a reliable narrator.

Therefore, the reader cannot judge what is real and what is imaginary. The ambiguity of the text suggests that the psychological state of the young Romantic protagonist may have an influence on her perceptions. Only if the reader considers what may be the governess's subconscious motives can he or she appreciate all the possible meanings of the story.

Pre-Reading Activities

1. What is the supernatural? Why do you think stories about the supernatural are popular?
2. What kind of setting or atmosphere would make for a good "ghost story"?

Key Terms

ambiguous meaning	good versus evil
consciousness	Gothic tale
double	indirect narration
framed story	literary conventions
Freud, Sigmund (1856–1939)	subconscious

From *The Turn of the Screw*
Henry James

The story had held us, round the fire, sufficiently breath-   1
less, but except the obvious remark that it was **gruesome**, as on
Christmas Eve in an old house a strange tale should essentially be, I
remember no comment **uttered** till somebody happened to note it as
the only case he had met in which . . . a [ghost's] visitation had
fallen on a child.

The case, I may mention, was that of an **apparition** in just   2
such an old house as had gathered us for the occasion—an appearance, of a dreadful kind, to a little boy sleeping in the room with his
mother and waking her up in the terror of it; waking her not to **dissipate** his dread and soothe him to sleep again, but to **encounter**
also herself . . . the same sight that had shocked him.

It was this observation that drew from Douglas—not immedi-   3
ately, but later in the evening—a reply that had the interesting con-

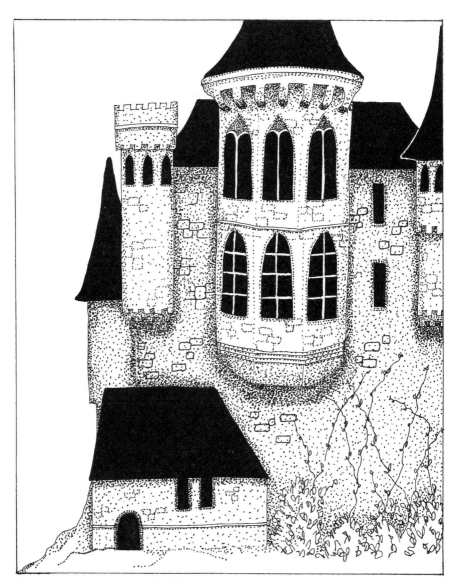

Figure 16 • European Gothic castle

sequence to which I call attention. Some one else told a story not
particularly effective, which I saw he was not following. This I took
for a sign that he had himself something to produce and that we
should only have to wait. We waited in fact till two nights later; but
that same evening, before we **scattered**, he brought out what was in
his mind.

"I quite agree—in regard to [that] ghost, or whatever it was   4
—that its appearing first to the little boy, at so **tender** an age, adds
a particular touch. But it's not the first occurrence of its charming kind that I know to have been concerned with a child. If the
child gives the effect another turn of the **screw**, what do you say to
two children—?"

"We say of course," somebody exclaimed, "that two children   5
give two turns! Also that we want to hear about them."

I can see Douglas there before the fire, to which he had got up   6
to present his back, looking down at this **converser** with his hands
in his pockets. "Nobody but me, till now, has ever heard. It's quite
too horrible." This was naturally declared by several voices to give
the thing the **utmost** price, and our friend, with quiet art, prepared
his triumph by turning his eyes over the rest of us and going on: "It's
beyond everything. Nothing at all that I know touches it."

"For sheer terror?" I remember asking.   7

He seemed to say it wasn't so simple as that; to be really at a   8
loss how to qualify it. He passed his hand over his eyes, made a little
wincing grimace. "For dreadful—dreadfulness!"

"Oh how delicious!" cried one of the women.   9

He took no notice of her; he looked at me, but as if, instead of   10
me, he saw what he spoke of. "For general **uncanny** ugliness and
horror and pain."

"Well, then," I said, "just sit right down and begin."   11

. . . Then as he faced us again: "I can't begin. I shall have to   12
send to town. . . . The story's written. It's in a locked drawer—it
has not been out for years. . . ."

"Your manuscript—?"   13

"Is in old faded ink and in the most beautiful **hand**." He **hung**   14
fire again. "A woman's. She has been dead these twenty years. She
sent me the pages in question before she died." They were all listening now. . . .

Let me say here distinctly, to **have done with** it, that this   15
narrative, from an exact transcript of my own made much later, is
what I shall presently give. Poor Douglas, before his death—when
it was in sight—**committed** to me the manuscript that reached him
. . . and with immense effort, he began to read to our **hushed** little
circle on the night of the fourth.

The departing ladies who had said they would stay didn't, of   16
course, thank heaven, stay: they departed, in consequence of arrange-
ments made, in a rage of curiosity . . . produced by the touches
with which he had already worked us up. But that only made his

little final **auditory** more compact and select, kept it, round the **hearth**, subject to a common thrill.

    . . . [H]is old friend, the youngest of several daughters of a   17
poor country **parson**, had at the age of twenty . . . come up to
London, in **trepidation**, to answer an advertisement. . . . [T]he
advertiser . . . proved . . . a gentleman, a bachelor in the **prime**
of life, such a figure as had never risen, save in a dream or an old
novel, before a **fluttered** anxious girl. . . . One could easily have
fixed his type; it never, happily, dies out. He was handsome and bold
and pleasant, off-hand and gay and kind. He struck her, **inevitably**,
as gallant and splendid . . . rich . . . in a glow of high fashion, of
good looks, of expensive habits, of charming ways with women. He
had for his town residence a big house filled with the **spoils** of travels and trophies of the **chase**; but it was to his country home, an old
family place in Essex, that he wished her immediately to proceed.

    He had been left . . . **guardian** to a small nephew [named   18
Miles] and a small niece [named Flora] . . . [whom he had] . . .
sent . . . down to his other house, the proper place for them being
the country. . . .

    There had been for the two children at first a young lady   19
whom they had had the misfortune to lose. She **had done for**
them quite beautifully—she was a most respectable person—till her
death. . . .

    So far had Douglas presented his picture when some one put a   20
question. "And what did the former governess die of? Of so much
respectability?"

    Our friend's answer was prompt. "That will come out. I don't   21
anticipate."

    "Pardon me—I thought that was just what you *are* doing."   22

    . . ."You shall hear tomorrow what she learnt. Meanwhile of   23
course the prospect struck her as slightly **grim**. She was young, un-
tried, nervous: it was a vision of serious duties and little company, of
really great loneliness. . . . But the salary offered much exceeded
her modest measure, and on a second interview, she **faced the music**, she **engaged**. . . . [H]is main condition was that she should
never trouble him—but never, never: neither appeal nor complain
nor write about anything . . . let him alone. She promised to do
this, and she mentioned to me that when, for a moment, **disburdened**, delighted, he held her hand, thanking her for the sacrifice,
she already felt rewarded."

    "But was that all her reward?" one of the ladies asked.   24
    "She never saw him again."   25

. . . Douglas had begun to read with a fine clearness that was   26
like a **rendering** to the ear of the beauty of his author's hand. . . .

[from the governess's tale]

[Some time after I arrived at the country house, Bly, I spent   27
the day with little Flora and arranged for her to show me the place.]
Young as she was I was struck, throughout our little tour, with her
confidence and courage, with the way, in empty chambers and dull
corridors, on crooked staircases that made me pause and even on the
summit of an old . . . square tower that made me dizzy, her morning music, her disposition to tell me so many more things than she
asked, rang out and led me on. I have not seen Bly since the day I
left it, and I dare say that to my present older and more informed
eyes, it would show a very reduced importance.

But as my little conductress, with her hair of gold and her   28
frock of blue, danced before me round the corners and pattered
down passages, I had the view of a castle of romance inhabited by a
rosy **sprite**, such a place as would somehow, for the diversion of the
young idea, take all color out of story-books and fairy-tales. Wasn't it
just a story-book over which I had fallen [asleep] and a-dream? No;
it was a big ugly antique but convenient house, embodying a few features of a building still older, half-displaced and half-used, in which I
had the fancy of our being almost as lost as a handful of passengers in
a great drifting ship. Well, I was strangely at the helm!

. . . One afternoon, . . . the children were tucked away and   29
I had come out for my stroll. One of the thoughts that, as I don't in
the least shrink now from noting, used to be with me in these
wanderings was that it would be as charming as a charming story
suddenly to meet someone. Some one would appear there at the
turn of a path and would stand before me and smile and approve. I
didn't ask more than that—I only asked that he should *know*; and
the only way to be sure he knew would be to see it, and the kind
light of it, in his handsome face. . . . What arrested me on the
spot—and with a shock much greater than any vision had allowed
for—was the sense that my imagination had, in a flash, turned real.
He did stand there!—but high up, beyond the lawn and at the very
top of the tower to which, on that first morning, little Flora had conducted me. . . .

It produced in me, this figure, in the clear twilight, I remem-   30
ber, two distinct gasps of emotion, which were, sharply, the shock of
my first and that of my second surprise. My second was a violent per-

ception of the mistake of my first: the man who met my eyes was not the man I expected, but . . . an unknown man.

The place, moreover, in the strangest way in the world, had on 31 the instant and by the very fact of its appearance become a solitude . . . . It was as if, while I took in what I did take in, all the rest of the scene had been stricken with death. I can hear again, as I write, the intense hush in which the sounds of evening dropped. The **rooks** stopped cawing in the golden sky and the friendly hour lost for the unspeakable minute all its voice. But there was no other change in nature, unless indeed it were a change that I saw with a stranger sharpness. The gold was still in the sky, the clearness in the air, and the man who looked at me over the battlements was as definite as a picture in a frame. That's how I thought, with extraordinary quickness, of each person he might have been and that he wasn't.

He was in one of the angles, the one away from the house, 32 very erect, as it struck me, and with both hands on the ledge. So I saw him as I see the letters I form on this page; then, exactly, after a minute . . . he slowly changed his place—passed, looking at me hard all the while, to the opposite corner of the platform. Yes, it was intense to me that during this transit he never took his eyes from me, and I can see at this moment the way his hand, as he went, moved from one of the **crenellations** to the next. He stopped at the other corner, but less long, and even as he turned away still markedly fixed me. He turned away; that was all I knew.

Vocabulary

anticipate *(v.)*   to speak or write in knowledge or expectation of something to come
apparition *(n.)*   ghostly figure
***auditory** *(n.)*   audience
chase *(n.)*   hunt
commit *(v.)*   to give in charge or trust; to entrust
***converser** *(n.)*   one who is talking or carrying on a conversation
***crenellation** *(n.)*   upthrust portion of a battlement (a wall used for defense on top of a castle, fort, or tower)
***disburdened** *(adj.)*   unburdened; unworried
dissipate *(v.)*   to dispel
***do [for]** *(v.)*   to care [for]

*Denotes low-frequency word.

encounter *(v.)*   to meet
***engage** *(v.)*   to agree to employment
face the music *(v. phrase)*   to meet an unpleasant situation directly
***fluttered** *(adj.)*   agitated; disturbed
grim *(adj.)*   frightful; sinister
grimace *(n.)*   facial expression usually of disgust or disapproval
gruesome *(adj.)*   inspiring horror or repulsion
guardian *(n.)*   person legally placed in charge of the affairs of a minor
***hand** *(n.)*   handwriting
hang fire *(v.)*   to hesitate
***have done with [it]** *(v. phrase)*   to bring [something] to an end
hearth *(n.)*   area in front of a fireplace
hushed *(adj.)*   quiet
inevitably *(adv.)*   inescapably; unavoidably
***parson** *(n.)*   clergyman or minister in charge of a parish
prime *(n.)*   most active, thriving, or successful period
***rendering** *(n.)*   imparting; giving
***rook** *(n.)*   large, crowlike bird
scatter *(v.)*   to go in various directions; to disperse
screw *(n.)*   spirally grooved pin used to fasten parts of something
     together; also, instrument of torture applied to the thumbs of a
     prisoner. Both meanings are intended here.
spoils *(n., usually pl.)*   goods or objects resulting from a special effort
***sprite** *(n.)*   small supernatural being
tender *(adj.)*   young
trepidation *(n.)*   apprehension
uncanny *(adj.)*   strange; weird
utmost *(adj.)*   highest; greatest
uttered *(adj.)*   spoken
wincing *(adj.)*   flinching; shrinking back

Activities

1. Reread the story closely, noting in your journal the setting and atmo-
    sphere that James creates. What specific vocabulary does he use to cre-
    ate these? Discuss your ideas with your group.
2. Who is James's audience for the story within the story? How does
    James secure their attention?
3. What is the governess like? What images show her state of mind?
    Why might a Freudian psychologist doubt the governess's story?
4. Discuss what you think is the meaning of the title of the story.

*Denotes low-frequency word.

5. Write an essay summarizing the important qualities of a good ghost story.

6. A complex structure is typical of many modern stories and novels. Look closely at how James has assembled *The Turn of the Screw*. Who is telling the story? Make notes in your journal and discuss your findings with your group.

7. Based on your notes and your discussion, write an essay on the complex structure of *The Turn of the Screw*.

8. Using your imagination, write an ending to *The Turn of the Screw*. Be sure to use the characters introduced by James. (Note that the governess has no name.)

For Further Reading

Edel, Leon. *Henry James: A Life.* New York: Harper, 1985.

MacAndrew, Elizabeth. *The Gothic Tradition in Fiction.* New York: Columbia UP, 1979.

Purdy, Strother B. *The Hole in the Fabric: Science, Contemporary Literature, and Henry James.* Pittsburgh: U of Pittsburgh P, 1977.

Schug, Charles. *The Romantic Genesis of the Modern Novel.* Pittsburgh: U of Pittsburgh P, 1979.

13

From *Uncle Vanya*

Anton Chekhov (1860–1904)
Drama: Comedy

Background

At the end of the nineteenth century, most of the writers in Russia were members of the nobility. However, Anton Chekhov came from a family of emancipated serfs—that is, his forefathers had been bound to their masters' land but were later freed. In spite of his modest background, Chekhov succeeded in getting an education. While he was studying medicine at Moscow University, he supported himself and his family by writing comic stories.

Chekhov practiced medicine throughout his life. His medical training and professional experiences provided him with a scientific, objective view of the world. Furthermore, as a doctor he met many types of people, and he lived in the environments of both the city and the countryside. These varied experiences were incorporated as realistic details into Chekhov's works.

Although Chekhov wrote more than 50 stories, he is best remembered for his dramas *The Sea Gull* (1896), *Uncle Vanya* (1899), *The Three Sisters* (1902), and *The Cherry Orchard* (1904). These plays have earned Chekhov a reputation as an outstanding representative of the late-nineteenth-century Realist school. His observations of Russian life are presented on stage in a spare and concentrated form. With dramatic characters representing diverse classes, professions, and individual personalities, Chekhov's work provides a panoramic view of the Russia of his time.

Pre-Reading Activities

1. In your journal, note your ideas about life in the country as opposed to life in the city. Which do you think is preferable? Why? Discuss your ideas with your group.
2. Why do you believe science and social traditions sometimes come into conflict? What do you think might be the result?

Key Terms

czar/czarist Russia	Naturalism
Flaubert, Gustave (1821–1880)	objectivity
indirect method	serf
Maupassant, Guy de (1850–1893)	Tolstoy, Leo (1828–1910)
Moscow Art Theater	Zola, Émile (1840–1902)

From *Uncle Vanya*
Anton Chekhov

Characters for This Scene

ALEXANDER SEREBRAKOFF, a retired professor

SONIA, his daughter by a former marriage

IVAN [VANYA] VOITSKI, son of a **privy councilor** and brother-in-law to Serebrakoff

MICHAEL ASTROFF, a medical doctor

ILIA [WAFFLES] TELEGIN, an **impoverished** landowner

MARINA, an old nurse

The scene is laid on Serebrakoff's country place.

Act I

A country house on a terrace. In front of it, a garden. In an avenue of trees, under an old poplar, stands a table set for tea, with a **samovar**, etc. Some benches and chairs stand near the table. On one of them is lying a guitar. A **hammock** is swung near the table. It is three o'clock in the afternoon of a cloudy day. MARINA, a quiet, gray-haired, little old woman, is sitting at the table knitting a stocking. ASTROFF is walking up and down near her.

Figure 17 • Around the samovar, late nineteenth century *(Culver Pictures, Inc.)*

ASTROFF: . . . [T]en years have made me another man. And why? Because I am overworked. Nurse, I am on my feet from dawn till dusk. I know no rest; at night I **tremble** under my blankets for fear of being dragged out to visit one who is sick; I have **toiled** without **repose** or a day's freedom since I have known you; could I help growing old? And then, existence is tedious, anyway; it is a senseless, dirty business, this life, and goes heavily. Every one about here is silly, and after living with them for two or three years one grows silly oneself. It is inevitable. [*Twisting his mustache*] See what a long mustache I have grown. A foolish, long mustache. Yes, I am as silly as the rest, nurse, but not as stupid; no, I have not grown stupid. Thank God, my brain is not **addled** yet, though my feelings have grown **numb**. I ask nothing, I need nothing, I love no one, unless it is yourself alone. [*He kisses her head*] I had a nurse just like you when I was a child.

MARINA: Don't you want a bite of something to eat?

ASTROFF: No. During the third week of **Lent** I went to the epidemic at Malitskoi. It was . . . **typhoid**. The peasants were all lying side by side in their huts, and the calves and pigs were running about the floor among the sick. Such dirt there was, and smoke!   20
Unspeakable! I slaved among those people all day, not a crumb passed my lips, but when I got home there was still no rest for me; a switchman was carried in from the railroad; I laid him on the operating table and he went and died in my arms under **chloroform**, and then my feelings that should have been dead awoke again, my   25
conscience tortured me as if I had killed the man. I sat down and closed my eyes—like this—and thought: will our descendants two hundred years from now, for whom we are breaking the road, remember to give us a kind word? No, nurse, they will forget.

MARINA: Man is forgetful, but God remembers.   30

ASTROFF: Thank you for that. You have spoken the truth.

[*Enter* VOITSKI *from the house. He has been asleep after dinner and looks rather **disheveled**. He sits down on the bench and straightens his collar*]

VOITSKI: H'm. Yes. [*A pause*] Yes.

ASTROFF: Have you been asleep?

VOITSKI: Yes, very much so. [*He yawns*] Ever since the professor and his wife have come, our daily life seems to have jumped the track. I   35
sleep at the wrong time, drink wine, and eat all sorts of messes for luncheon and dinner. It isn't **wholesome**. . . .

MARINA [*shakes her head*]: Such a confusion in the house! The professor gets up at twelve, the samovar is kept boiling all the morning and everything has to wait for him. Before they came we used to   40
have dinner at one o'clock, like everybody else, but now we have it at seven. The professor sits up all night writing and reading, and suddenly, at two o'clock, there goes the bell! Heavens, what is that? The professor wants some tea! Wake the servants, light the samovar! Lord, what disorder!   45

ASTROFF: Will they be here long?

VOITSKI: A hundred years! The professor has decided to make his home here.

MARINA: Look at this now! The samovar has been on the table for two hours, and they are all out walking!   50

VOITSKI: All right, don't get excited; here they come.

[*Voices are heard approaching.* SEREBRAKOFF, SONIA, *and* TELEGIN *come in from the depths of the garden, returning from their walk*]

SEREBRAKOFF: Superb! Superb! What beautiful views!

TELEGIN: They are wonderful, your Excellency.

SONIA: Tomorrow we shall go into the woods, shall we, papa?

VOITSKI: Ladies and gentlemen, tea is ready.   55

SEREBRAKOFF: Won't you please be good enough to send my tea into the library? I still have some work to finish.

SONIA: I am sure you will love the woods.

[. . . SEREBRAKOFF *and* SONIA *go into the house*]

VOITSKI: There goes our learned scholar on a hot, **sultry** day like this, in his overcoat and **galoshes** and carrying an umbrella!   60

ASTROFF: He is trying to take good care of his health. . . .

ASTROFF: Come, Ivan, tell us something.

VOITSKI: [*indolently*] What shall I tell you?

ASTROFF: Haven't you any news for us?

VOITSKI: No, it is all **stale**. I am just the same as usual, or perhaps   65
worse, because I have become lazy. I don't do anything now but **croak** like an old **raven**. My mother, the old **magpie**, is still **chattering** about the **emancipation** of woman, with one eye on her grave and the other on her **learned** books, in which she is always looking for the dawn of a new life.   70

ASTROFF: And the professor?

VOITSKI: The professor sits in his library from morning till night, as usual—

> **Straining** the mind, **wrinkling** the **brow**,
> We write, write, write,   75
> Without **respite**
> Or hope of praise in the future or now.

Poor paper! He ought to write his autobiography; he would make a really splendid subject for a book! Imagine it, the life of a retired professor, as stale as a piece of hardtack, tortured by gout, headaches,   80
and rheumatism, his liver bursting with jealousy and envy, living on the estate of his first wife, although he hates it, because he can't afford to live in town. He is **everlastingly whining** about his hard lot, though, as a matter of fact, he is extraordinarily lucky. He is the son of a common **deacon** and has attained the professor's chair,   85

become the son-in-law of a senator, is called "your Excellency,"
and so on. But I'll tell you something; the man has been writing on
art for twenty-five years, and he doesn't know the very first thing
about it. For twenty-five years he has been chewing on other
men's thoughts about realism, naturalism, and all such foolishness;   90
for twenty-five years he has been reading and writing things that
clever men have long known and stupid ones are not interested in;
for twenty-five years he has been **making** his imaginary **mountains out of molehills**. And just think of the man's self-conceit
and presumption all this time! For twenty-five years he has been   95
masquerading in false clothes and has now retired, absolutely
unknown to any living soul; and yet see him! **stalking** across the
earth like a **demi-god**!

ASTROFF: I believe you envy him.

VOITSKI: Yes, I do. Look at the success he has had with women! . . .   100
His first wife, who was my sister, was a beautiful, gentle being. . . .
His mother-in-law, my mother, adores him to this day. . . . His
second wife is, as you see, a brilliant beauty, she married him in his
old age and has surrendered all the glory of her beauty and freedom to him. Why? What for?   105

ASTROFF: Is she faithful to him?

VOITSKI: Yes, unfortunately she is.

ASTROFF: Why "unfortunately"?

VOITSKI: Because such fidelity is false and unnatural, **root and branch**.
It sounds [good], but there is no logic in it. It is thought immoral   110
for a woman to deceive an old husband whom she hates, but quite
moral for her to strangle her youth in her breast and **banish** every
vital desire from her heart.

TELEGIN [*in a tearful voice*]: Vanya, I don't like to hear you talk so. Listen,
Vanya; every one who betrays husband or wife is faithless, and   115
could also betray his country.

VOITSKI [*crossly*]: **Turn off the tap**, Waffles.

Vocabulary

*addle (*v.*)   to confuse
banish (*v.*)   to drive out

---

*Denotes low-frequency word.

brow *(n.)* forehead

chatter *(v.)* to talk rapidly or idly

*chloroform *(n.)* anesthesia used in earlier times to prevent pain during surgery

*croak *(v.)* to speak in a hoarse, throaty voice

*deacon *(n.)* subordinate officer in a Christian church

*demi-god *(n.)* person regarded as partly divine

disheveled *(adj.)* untidy; rumpled

emancipation *(n.)* freeing from the power or control of another

*everlastingly *(adv.)* eternally

*galoshes *(n.)* boots

*hammock *(n.)* swinging bed made of netting and hung from two poles

impoverished *(adj.)* made poor

*indolently *(adv.)* lazily

learned *(adj.)* having or showing good education

Lent *(n.)* the 40 weekdays from Ash Wednesday to Easter observed by Christians as a period of penitence and fasting

*magpie *(n.)* kind of bird that makes rapidly succeeding sounds; a person who talks in such a way

*make a mountain out of a molehill *(v. phrase)* to make more of something than is necessary or required

  *molehill *(n.)* little mound of dirt pushed up by a mole, an animal that lives underground

masquerade *(v.)* to go about disguised

numb *(adj.)* without feeling or emotion; deadened

*privy councilor *(n.)* confidential advisor appointed by a ruler

*raven *(n.)* large black bird

repose *(n.)* state of rest

respite *(n.)* interval of rest or relief

*root and branch *(adv.)* completely; entirely

*samovar *(n.)* metal container with an internal tube for heating water to make tea, used especially in Russia

stale *(adj.)* having lost freshness or originality

stalking *(adj.)* walking stiffly or haughtily

straining *(adj.)* exerting to the utmost

sultry *(adj.)* sweltering; hot and humid

toil *(v.)* to work long and hard

tremble *(v.)* to shake

*turn off the tap *(v. phrase)* to stop crying

  *tap *(n.)* spout and valve at the end of a pipe that control the flow of a liquid

*typhoid *(n.)* serious disease contracted from polluted water and marked by high fever

whine *(v.)* to complain in a childish, undignified way

wholesome *(adj.)* promoting health or well-being

wrinkling *(adj.)* creasing; making small ridges

Activities

1. Taking the parts of the characters, read the play aloud. Note the tensions and conflicts between the characters.

2. Alone or with a partner, look closely at the text. What does Voitski think of the professor? Why do you think he feels this way? Make notes in your journal about what he is saying about Russian education. Discuss your views with your class.

3. Describe the marriage between Professor Serebrakoff and his second wife. What does Voitski think of this marriage?

4. Like Chekhov, Astroff is a medical doctor. Make notes in your journal about his view of Russia. Share your ideas with your class.

5. How does living in the country affect Dr. Astroff? Do you think this is the usual effect it has on people? Why might he feel the way he does?

6. Write an essay on Chekhov's view of his contemporary Russia.

7. Do you think young women should marry older men? (These are sometimes called May-December marriages.) Write an essay defending your point of view.

8. If you have read "The Miller's Tale," compare and contrast the way Chaucer presents the marriages of John the Carpenter and Alison with the way Chekhov presents the marriage of Professor Serebrakoff and his second wife.

For Further Reading

Barricelli, Jean-Pierre, ed. *Chekhov's Great Plays: A Critical Anthology*. New York: New York UP, 1981.

Chekhov, Anton. *Anton Chekhov's Life and Thought: Selected Letters and Commentary*. Trans. Michael H. Heim with Simon Karlinsky. Berkeley: U of California P, 1975.

Jackson, Robert L., ed. *Chekhov*. Englewood Cliffs, NJ: Prentice, 1967.

Mechinger, Siegfried. *Anton Chekhov*. New York: Ungar, 1972.

Priestly, J. B. *Anton Chekhov*. Cranbury, NJ: Barnes, 1970.

14

From "Roman Fever"

Edith Wharton (1862–1937)
Fiction: Short Story

Background

Born in the North during the American Civil War, Edith Jones was fortunate enough to enjoy the luxuries of an old New York family. The Jones family went to Europe on what Americans called "the Grand Tour" and later stayed for prolonged visits. They spent summers vacationing at their large second home in Newport, Rhode Island. However, like most young women of her day, Edith received no formal education; her travels and her reading in her father's library formed the bases of her knowledge. Through her governess she learned German and French and thus was able to read great European literature in the original languages.

After her marriage to Edward Wharton in 1885, Edith traveled extensively to Greece, Italy, and other parts of Europe, as well as to North Africa. In 1891 she published her first short story, "The Bunner Sisters." Her 1897 book *The Decoration of Houses*, written with Ogden Codman, is still a classic on interior decoration.

Although she received the Pulitzer Prize in fiction for her novel *The Age of Innocence* (1921), Edith Wharton also excelled as a short-story writer. Her stories include Gothic tales as well as many more realistic ones, a number of which focus on the city of her birth, New York. Wharton left the United States in 1909 for permanent exile in Paris. But she continued to write critically of the nouveaux riches—that is, the newly rich Americans who made their fortunes on railroads and other developing industries and displaced the traditional Eastern aristocratic families. A close friend of Henry James, she frequently wrote on international themes, especially about Americans living in or visiting Europe.

While her fiction is usually considered realistic, it also contains many references to biblical, Greek, and Roman mythology. Understanding these references greatly expands the surface meaning of Wharton's fiction. It is important to note that in "Roman Fever" a dramatic dialogue between two goddesslike Americans takes place overlooking the ruins of Rome. Meanwhile, their innocent daughters have flown off to Tarquinia with two airplane pilots in Mussolini's Fascist air force. The ruins of the past hint at a sinister future both for the daughters and for Italy of the 1930s.

Pre-Reading Activities

1. With your study group, discuss the reasons why, in your opinion, a visitor would want to go to an ancient city such as Rome. What kinds of things might a visitor do and think about there?
2. How might an author show that two characters are different from each other? What techniques might she use?

Key Terms

Colosseum	irony
dramatic technique	nouveau riche (*pl.* nouveaux riches)
Etruscan	Palatine Hill
Fascism	Pulitzer Prize
Forum	Roman fever
the Grand Tour	Tarquinia
international themes	

From "Roman Fever"
Edith Wharton

From the table at which they had been lunching two American   1
ladies of ripe but well-cared-for middle age moved across the **lofty** terrace of the Roman restaurant and, leaning on its **parapet**, looked first at each other, and then down on the outspread glories of the Palatine and the Forum. . . .

As they leaned there a girlish voice echoed up gaily from the   2
stairs. . . . "Well, come along, then," it cried, not to them but to an invisible companion, "and let's leave the young things to their

Figure 18 • Roman Forum and Colosseum *(The Bettmann Archive)*

knitting . . . after all, we haven't left our poor parents much else to do. . . . "

"Barbara!" [the smaller and paler one] murmured, sending an unheard **rebuke** after the **mocking** voice in the stairway.   3

The other lady, who was fuller, and higher in color, with a small determined nose supported by vigorous black eyebrows, gave a good-humoured laugh. "That's what our daughters think of us!"   4

Her companion replied . . . , "Not of us individually. We must remember that. It's just the collective modern idea of Mothers. And you see—" Half guiltily she drew from her handsomely mounted black hand-bag a twist of crimson silk run through by fine knitting needles. "One never knows," she murmured. "The new system has certainly given us a good deal of **time to kill**; and sometimes I get tired just looking—even at this." Her gesture was now addressed to the **stupendous** scene at their feet. . . .   5

"Well, I don't see why we shouldn't just stay here," said Mrs. Slade, the lady of the high color and energetic brows. . . . "After all, it's still the most beautiful view in the world."   6

"It always will be, to me," assented her friend Mrs. Ansley,   7 with a slight stress on the "me" that Mrs. Slade, though she noticed it, wondered if it were not merely accidental. . . .

"Grace Ansley was always old-fashioned," she thought; and 8 added aloud, with a **retrospective** smile: "It's a view we've both been familiar with for a good many years. When we first met here we were younger than our girls are now. . . ."

[Alida] Slade's black brows drew together. . . . But she 9 smiled away her frown. . . . "Well, why not? We might do worse. There's no knowing, I suppose, when the girls will be back. Do you even know from *where*? I don't."

Mrs. Ansley again colored slightly. "I think those young Italian 10 aviators we met at the Embassy invited them to fly to Tarquinia for tea. I suppose they'll want to wait and fly back by moonlight."

"Moonlight—moonlight! What a part it still plays. Do you 11 suppose they're as sentimental as we were?"

"I've come to the conclusion that I don't in the least know 12 what they are," said Mrs. Ansley. "And perhaps we didn't know much more about each other."

. . . Each one, of course, had a label ready to attach to the 13 other's name; Mrs. Delphin Slade, for instance, would have told herself, or any one who asked her, that Mrs. Horace Ansley, twenty-five years ago, had been exquisitely lovely—no, you wouldn't believe it, would you? . . . though, of course, still charming, distinguished. . . . Well, as a girl she had been exquisite; far more beautiful than her daughter Barbara, though certainly **Babs**, according to the new standards at any rate, was more effective—had more *edge*, as they say. Funny where she got it, with those two **nullities** as parents. Yes; Horace Ansley was—well, the duplicate of his wife. . . .

A few years later, and not many months apart, both ladies 14 **lost their husbands**. . . . The similarity of their lot had again drawn them together. . . .

. . . [B]eing *the* Slade's widow was dullish business. . . . In 15 living up to such a husband all her **faculties** had been engaged; now she had only her daughter to live up to. . . . There was nothing left but to mother her daughter; and dear Jenny was such a perfect daughter that she needed no excessive mothering. . . . She wished that Jenny would fall in love—with the wrong man, even; that she might have to be watched, **outmaneuvered**, rescued. And instead, it was Jenny who watched her mother, kept her out of **draughts**, made sure she had taken her **tonic**. . . .

Mrs. Ansley was much less **articulate** than her friend, and her   16
mental portrait of Mrs. Slade was slighter, and drawn with fainter
touches. "Alida Slade's awfully brilliant; but not as brilliant as she
thinks," would have summed it up. . . .

"I was just thinking," [Mrs. Slade] said slowly, "what different   17
things Rome stands for to each generation of travellers. To our grandmothers, Roman fever; to our mothers, sentimental dangers—how
we used to be guarded!—to our daughters, no more dangers than
the middle of Main Street. They don't know it—but how much
they're missing!"

. . . "The sun's set. You're not afraid, my dear?" [said Mrs.   18
Slade].

"Afraid—"   19

"Of Roman fever or pneumonia? I remember how ill you were   20
that winter. As a girl you had a very delicate throat, hadn't you? . . .
There's no more Roman fever, but the Forum is deathly cold after
sunset—especially after a hot day. And the Colosseum's even colder
and damper."

"The Colosseum—?"   21

"Yes. It wasn't easy to get in, after the gates were locked for   22
the night. Far from easy. Still in those days it could be managed; it
was managed, often. Lovers met there who couldn't meet elsewhere.
You knew that?"

"I—I **daresay**. I don't remember."   23

"You don't remember? You don't remember going to visit some   24
ruins or other one evening, just after dark, and catching a bad chill?
People always said that expedition was what caused your illness."

There was a moment's silence; then Mrs. Ansley **rejoined**:   25
"Did they? It was all so long ago."

. . . "I've always known why you went. . . . Well, you   26
went to meet the man I was engaged to—and I can repeat every
word of the letter that took you there. . . . Listen, if you don't
believe me. 'My one darling, things can't go on like this. I must see
you alone. Come to the Colosseum immediately after dark tomorrow.
There will be somebody to let you in. No one whom you need fear
will suspect'—but perhaps you've forgotten what the letter said?"

Mrs. Ansley met the challenge with an unexpected **compo-**   27
sure. Steadying herself against the chair she looked at her friend,
and replied: "No; I know it by heart too."

"And the signature? 'Only *your* D.S.' Was that it? I'm right,   28
am I? That was the letter that took you out that evening after

dark? . . . Well, my dear, I know what was in that letter because I wrote it! . . . I hated you, hated you. I knew you were in love with Delphin—and I was afraid; afraid of you, of your quiet ways, your sweetness . . . your . . . well, I wanted you out of the way, that's all. Just for a few weeks; just till I was sure of him. . . . I had no reason to think you'd ever taken it seriously. How could I, when you were married to Horace Ansley two months afterward? As soon as you could get out of bed your mother rushed you off to Florence and married you. . . ."

At length Mrs. Slade began again: "I suppose I did it as a sort of joke—" 29

"A joke?" 30

"Well, girls are ferocious sometimes, you know. Girls in love 31 especially. And I remember laughing to myself all that evening at the idea that you were waiting around there in the dark. . . . Of course I was upset when I heard you were so ill afterward."

Mrs. Ansley had not moved for a long time. But now she 32 turned slowly toward her companion. "But I didn't wait. He'd arranged everything. He was there. We were let in at once," she said. . . . "I answered the letter. I told him I'd be there. So he came."

Mrs. Slade **flung** her hands up to her face. "Oh, God—you 33 answered! I never thought of your answering. . . ."

"It's odd you never thought of it, if you wrote the letter." 34

. . . Mrs. Ansley rose, and drew her fur scarf about her. "It is 35 cold here. We'd better go. . . . I'm sorry for you," she said. . . .

The unexpected words sent a **pang** through Mrs. Slade. "Yes; 36 we'd better go." She gathered up her bag and cloak. "I don't know why you should be sorry for me," she muttered.

Mrs. Ansley stood looking away from her toward the **dusky** 37 secret mass of the Colosseum. "Well—because I didn't have to wait that night."

Mrs. Slade gave an unquiet laugh. "Yes; I was beaten there. 38 But I oughtn't to **begrudge** it to you, I suppose. At the end of all these years. After all, I had everything; I had him for twenty-five years. And you had nothing but that one letter that he didn't write."

Mrs. Ansley was again silent. At length she turned toward the 39 door of the terrace. She took a step, and turned back, facing her companion.

"I had Barbara," she said, and began to move ahead of Mrs. 40 Slade toward the stairway.

Vocabulary

articulate *(adj.)*   able to express oneself readily, clearly, and effectively
*Babs *(prop. n.)*   short for *Barbara*
begrudge *(v.)*   to look upon with disapproval
composure *(n.)*   calmness
*daresay *(v.)*   to suppose
*draught *(n.)*   a current of air (chiefly British; a variation of *draft*)
*dusky *(adj.)*   shadowy
faculty *(n.)*   ability
fling (flung) *(v.)*   to move suddenly
lofty *(adj.)*   impressively high
lose someone *(v.)*   to have someone who is close die
mocking *(adj.)*   ridiculing; treating with contempt
*nullity *(n.)*   something that has no value or significance
outmaneuver *(v.)*   to defeat by more skillful manipulation or management
pang *(n.)*   sharp attack of pain
*parapet *(n.)*   wall or railing to protect people from falling off the edge, as on a balcony or terrace
rebuke *(n.)*   expression of strong disapproval; reprimand
rejoin *(v.)*   to say in response
retrospective *(adj.)*   looking back to the past
steady oneself *(v.)*   to make oneself stable or fixed
stupendous *(adj.)*   overwhelming; astonishingly great
time to kill *(n.)*   time to waste or to use up
*tonic *(n.)*   medicine

Activities

1. What is the setting for the story "Roman Fever"? What is the Colosseum? Why is it important to the story?

2. Wharton carefully builds her story to show us what her characters are like. Find specific lines in "Roman Fever" that tell us about these two characters, and note them in your journal. Discuss your ideas with your class.

3. Look at the structure of the short story. How does the author show us what Mrs. Slade and Mrs. Ansley are like?

4. Based on your notes and classroom discussion, write an essay comparing and contrasting Mrs. Slade and Mrs. Ansley.

*Denotes low-frequency word.

5. Write an essay on the multiple meanings of "Roman fever." Include the significance of "Roman fever" to the three generations involved in the story.

For Further Reading

Fryer, Judith. *Felicitous Space: The Imaginative Structures of Edith Wharton and Willa Cather.* Chapel Hill: U of North Carolina P, 1986.

Lewis, R. W. B. *Edith Wharton: A Biography.* New York: Harper, 1975.

McDowell, Margaret B. *Edith Wharton.* Boston: Twayne, 1976.

Wolff, Cynthia Griffin. *A Feast of Words: The Triumph of Edith Wharton.* New York: Oxford, 1977.

CHAPTER **15**

From "The Metamorphosis"

Franz Kafka (1883–1924)
Fiction: Short Story

Background

Although he died at an early age, Kafka wrote many novels, novellas, and short prose pieces. Among his most well-known works are *The Trial* (1925), *The Castle* (1926), *America* (1927), and "The Metamorphosis" (1912). He is regarded as one of the great modern writers because of his psychoanalytic approach—that is, his deep exploration of the psychology of his characters.

Kafka's fiction reflects his strong sense of isolation and melancholy as a German-speaking Jew in Prague, Czechoslovakia, and as the artist son of an overbearing father who wished his son to become a businessman. Fathers and other authority figures play an important role in his stories, especially in the mind of the main character. Frequently, the protagonist is a young male ridden with feelings of guilt who is being judged by the powerful father figure.

The influence of Freud's psychoanalysis and his concept of the "Oedipus complex" is evident in both the content and the tone of Kafka's work. With the voice of a matter-of-fact narrator that reveals the inner workings of his character's mind, Kafka explores a bizarre world that still shocks modern readers.

"The Metamorphosis" is the story of Gregor Samsa, a traveling salesman who has been working very hard at a boring job to support his parents and sister. In Existential terms, his life is meaningless. One morning he awakens and believes himself transformed into a huge insect. He is confined to his room as much as possible. He is persecuted by his father; his mother pleads for him; his sister tries to feed him. After much suffering, to the relief of his family, Gregor dies.

As a comic tragedy about the isolation, alienation, inadequacy, and guilt of modern life, "The Metamorphosis" has become one of the most widely read and discussed works of twentieth-century literature.

Pre-Reading Activities

1. Discuss what influence you think a very strong father figure might have on a young man. How do you think the young man might rebel?

2. What techniques might an author use to reveal the innermost thoughts of a character? Would we know whether or not these thoughts were "normal"? How?

Key Terms

alienation
Austro-Hungarian Empire
Existentialism
Freud, Sigmund (1856–1939)
isolation
metaphor

Prague Circle
psychoanalysis
psychology
subconscious
vermin

From "The Metamorphosis"
Franz Kafka

As Gregor Samsa awoke one morning from uneasy dreams he   1
found himself transformed in his bed into a gigantic insect. He was lying on his hard, as it were **armor-plated**, back and when he lifted his head a little he could see his **dome-like** brown belly divided into stiff arched segments on top of which the bed quilt could hardly keep in position and was about to slide off completely. His numerous legs, which were pitifully thin compared to the rest of his **bulk**, waved helplessly before his eyes.

What has happened to me? he thought. It was no dream. His   2
room, a regular human bedroom, only rather too small, lay quiet between the four familiar walls. Above the table on which a collection

of cloth samples was unpacked and spread out—Samsa was a **commercial traveler**—hung the picture which he had recently cut out of an illustrated magazine and put into a pretty **gilt** frame. It showed a lady, with a fur cap on and a fur **stole**, sitting upright and holding out to the spectator a huge fur **muff** into which the whole of her arm had vanished!

Gregor's eyes turned next to the window, and the overcast sky—one could hear rain drops beating on the window gutter—made him quite melancholy. What about sleeping a little longer and forgetting all this nonsense, he thought, but it could not be done, for he was accustomed to sleeping on his right side and in his present condition he could not turn himself over. However violently he forced himself towards his right side he always rolled on his back again. He tried it at least a hundred times, shutting his eyes to keep from seeing his struggling legs, and only **desisted** when he began to feel in his side a faint dull ache he had never experienced before. . . .

He slid down again into his former position. This getting up early, he thought, makes one quite stupid. A man needs his sleep. Other commercials live like **harem women**. For instance, when I come back to the hotel [in the] morning to write up the orders I've got, these others are only sitting down to breakfast. Let me just try that with my chief; I'd be **sacked on the spot**. Anyhow, that might be quite a good thing for me, who can tell? If I didn't have to hold my hand because of my parents, I'd have **given notice** long ago, I'd have gone to the chief and told him exactly what I think of him. . . . For the moment, though, I'd better get up, since my train goes at five.

He looked at the alarm clock ticking on the chest. Heavenly Father! he thought. It was half-past six o'clock and the hands were quietly moving on, it was even past the half-hour, it was getting on toward a quarter to seven. Had the alarm clock not gone off? From the bed one could see that it had been properly set for four o'clock; of course it must have gone off. . . .

But what was he to do now? The next train went at seven o'clock; to catch that he would need to hurry like mad and his samples weren't even packed up, and he himself wasn't feeling particularly fresh and active. And even if he did catch the train he wouldn't avoid a **row** with the chief, since the firm's porter would have been waiting for the five o'clock train and would have long since reported his failure to turn up. The porter was a creature of the chief's, **spineless** and stupid. Well, supposing he were to say he was sick? But that would be most unpleasant and would look suspicious, since during his five years' employment he had not been ill once. . . .

As all this was running through his mind at top speed without   7
his being able to decide to leave his bed—the alarm clock had just struck a quarter to seven—there came a cautious tap at the door behind the head of his bed. "Gregor," said a voice—it was his mother's—"it's a quarter to seven. Hadn't you a train to catch?" That gentle voice!

Gregor had a shock as he heard his own voice answering hers,   8
unmistakably his own voice, it was true, but with a persistent horrible **twittering squeak** behind it like an undertone. . . . Gregor wanted to answer at length, but in the circumstances he confined himself to saying: "Yes, yes, thank you, Mother, I'm getting up now."

The wooden door between them must have kept the change   9
in his voice from being noticeable outside, for his mother contented herself with this statement and **shuffled** away. Yet this brief exchange of words had made the other members of the family aware that Gregor was still in the house, as they had not expected, and at one of the side doors his father was already knocking, gently, yet with his fist. "Gregor, Gregor," he called, "what's the matter with you?" And after a little while he called again in a deeper voice: "Gregor! Gregor!" At the other side door his sister was saying in a low, **plaintive** tone: "Gregor? Aren't you well? Are you needing anything?"

He answered them both at once: "I'm just ready," and did his   10
best to make his voice sound as normal as possible by enunciating the words very clearly. . . . His immediate intention was to get up quietly without being disturbed, to put on his clothes and above all eat his breakfast, and only then to consider what else was to be done, since in bed, he was well aware, his meditations would come to no sensible conclusion. . . .

"Gregor," said his father now from the left-hand room, "the   11
chief clerk has come and wants to know why you didn't catch the early train. We don't know what to say to him. Besides, he wants to talk to you in person. So open the door, please. He will be good enough to excuse the **untidiness** of your room."

"Good morning, Mr. Samsa," the chief clerk was calling **ami-   12
ably** meanwhile. "He's not well," said his mother to the visitor, while his father was still speaking through the door, "he's not well, sir, believe me. What else would make him miss a train! The boy thinks about nothing but his work. It makes me almost **cross** the way he never goes out in the evenings; he's been here the last eight days and

has stayed at home every single evening. He just sits there quietly at the table reading a newspaper or looking through railway timetables. The only amusement he gets is doing **fretwork**. For instance, he spent two or three evenings cutting out a little picture frame; you would be surprised to see how pretty it is; it's hanging in his room; you'll see it in a minute when Gregor opens the door. . . . "

"Well, can the chief clerk come in now?" asked Gregor's father   13
impatiently, again knocking on the door. "No," said Gregor. In the left-hand room a painful silence followed this refusal; in the right-hand room his sister began to **sob**. . . .

[W]hy was she crying? Because he wouldn't get up and let the   14
the chief clerk in, because he was in danger of losing his job, and because the chief would begin **dunning** his parents again for the old debts? Surely these were things one didn't need to worry about for the present. Gregor was still at home and not in the least thinking of **deserting** his family. At the moment, true, he was lying on the carpet and no one who knew the condition he was in could seriously expect him to **admit** the chief clerk. . . . And it seemed to Gregor that it would be much more sensible to leave him in peace for the present than to trouble him with tears and **entreaties**.

Vocabulary

admit *(v.)*   to allow to enter
amiably *(adv.)*   in a friendly manner; sociably
***armor-plated** *(adj.)*   covered with defensive material or protective covering such as is used in combat
bulk *(n.)*   massive size
***commercial traveler** *(n.)*   nineteenth-century traveling salesman
***cross** *(adj.)*   marked by bad temper; grumpy
deserting *(n.)*   leaving; abandoning
desist *(v.)*   to stop
***dome-like** *(adj.)*   arched
dun *(v.)*   to make persistent demands for payment
entreaty *(n.)*   plea; earnest request
***fretwork** *(n.)*   kind of ornamental work
gilt *(adj.)*   made of gold; gold-colored
***give notice** *(v.)*   to announce to an employer that one is going to leave a position

*Denotes low-frequency word.

*harem women *(n.)* women living together in an isolated room, as in a
    Muslim household
*muff *(n.)* tube-shaped warm covering for women's hands, often made
    of fur
on the spot *(adv.)* immediately; at once
plaintive *(adj.)* expressive of suffering or melancholy
*row *(n.)* quarrel; argument
*sack *(v.)* to dismiss or fire from a position
shuffle *(v.)* to walk in a sliding, dragging manner without lifting the feet
sob *(v.)* to cry with a catching of the breath
spineless *(adj.)* lacking strength of character
squeak *(n.)* sharp, shrill cry or sound
stole *(n.)* long, wide scarf worn by women, usually across the shoulders
twittering *(adj.)* trembling; quivering
untidiness *(n.)* disorder; disorganized state

Activities

1. From whose point of view is the story told? Do we know whether it is
    true or not?

2. Look closely at the text. How does Kafka make full use of the central
    metaphor (the insect) in his story? Make notes in your journal and
    discuss your ideas with your group or class.

3. What is Gregor's relationship with his family? What is his relationship
    with figures of authority besides his parents? Do you believe this is
    normal? Note lines from the text that support your view.

4. Using your notes, write an essay on Kafka's use of metaphor to show
    Gregor Samsa's suffering.

5. Write an essay arguing for or against a young person's taking a job se-
    lected by his/her parents.

For Further Reading

Anderson, Mark, ed. *Reading Kafka: Prague, Politics, and the Fin de Siècle.* New
    York: Schocken, 1989.

Carrouges, Michel. *Kafka versus Kafka.* University: U of Alabama P, 1962.

Robertson, Ritchie. *Kafka: Judaism, Politics, and Literature.* New York: Oxford
    UP, 1987.

Sandbank, Shimon. *After Kafka: The Influence of Kafka's Fiction.* Athens: U of
    Georgia P, 1989.

*Denotes low-frequency word.

16

From *O Pioneers!*

Willa Cather (1873–1947)
Fiction: Novel

Background

Although she was born in Virginia, Willa Cather and her extended family moved to the Nebraska prairie in 1883 during the great nineteenth-century migration to the American West. The stark contrast between the older, more settled East and the open prairie of Nebraska made a lasting impression on the developing author. For Cather, the Midwest landscape possessed an almost mystical quality; she associated its richness and productivity with ancient myths of fertility gods and goddesses. The land and its magical powers became the setting for many of her novels.

While growing up in the Midwest, Willa Cather strongly identified with masculine tradition. Sometimes calling herself William, Cather wore extremely short hair and dressed in men's clothing. However, her nonconformist appearance did not hide her talents. Cather attended the University of Nebraska, where she began writing reviews of cultural events for newspapers. Convinced that she could earn a living as a writer, Cather took a magazine job in Pittsburgh, Pennsylvania, in 1896. Ten years later, she moved to New York, where she worked for *McClure's Magazine*.

Especially in her early work, Cather values the Romantic ideal of the exalted individual and his sensations and impressions. Under the guidance of the American writer Sarah Orne Jewett, Cather learned that one can seek universal truths in the particular experience and that one person's struggle to survive can symbolize human efforts everywhere.

In 1923, Cather received the Pulitzer Prize in fiction for *One of Ours*, her World War I novel, which demonstrates a woman's view of war and its mindless destruction of idealistic youth. But her most memorable heroine is Alexandra Bergson, the protagonist of her 1913 novel *O Pioneers!* The story takes its title from Walt Whitman's poem "Pioneers! O Pioneers!" and is a combination of two short stories Cather had written: one the tragic love story of Marie Shabata and Emil Bergson, and the other the saga of the Bergson family and their relationship with the land. Unmarried and alone for much of the novel, Alexandra Bergson directs her reproductive energies into the land. But her imagination of the powers of the land reminds her of her own body's needs. *O Pioneers!* is Cather's most popular novel; in 1992 it was made into a television film. This portion of the novel is from Part III, "Winter Memories."

Pre-Reading Activities

1. With your class or study group, define *pioneer*. What do you imagine the personality of a pioneer might be like?
2. In your journal, make a list of your ideas about "the myth of the American West." Discuss your ideas with your class.

Key Terms

American Midwest   personification
corn god   prairie
Great (or Continental) Divide   saga
journalist   sod house
migration

From *O Pioneers!*
Willa Cather

Winter has settled down over the **Divide** again; the season in   1
which Nature **recuperates**, in which she sinks to sleep between the
fruitfulness of autumn and the passion of spring. The birds have
gone. The **teeming** life that goes on down in the long grass is **exterminated**. The prairie-dog keeps in his hole. The rabbits run **shivering** from one frozen garden patch to another. . . .

The **variegated** fields are all one color now; the pastures, the   2
stubble, the roads, the sky are the same leaden gray. The
hedgerows and trees are scarcely **perceptible** against the bare
earth, whose **slaty hue** they have taken on. . . . It is like an iron
country, and the spirit is oppressed by its rigor and melancholy. One

Figure 19 • Sod house on the American prairie, Nebraska, 1892 *(Historical Pictures Service)*

could easily believe that in that dead landscape the germs of life and fruitfulness were extinct forever. . . .

Marie sat sewing or crocheting . . . but she was always   3
thinking about the fields outside . . . where the snow was falling and packing. . . . She seemed to feel the weight of all the snow that lay down there. The branches had become so hard that they wounded your hand if you tried to break a twig. And yet, down under the frozen **crusts**, at the roots of the trees, the secret of life was still safe, warm as the blood in one's heart; and the spring would come again! Oh, it would come again!

If Alexandra had had much imagination she might have guessed   4
what was going on in Marie's mind, and she would have seen long before what was going on in [brother] Emil's. But that, as Emil himself had more than once **reflected**, was Alexandra's blind side, and her life had not been of the kind to sharpen her vision. Her training had all been toward the end of making her **proficient** in what she had undertaken to do.

Her personal life, her own realization of herself, was almost a   5
subconscious existence; like an underground river that came to the surface only here and there, at intervals months apart, and then sank again to flow on under her own fields. Nevertheless, the underground stream was there, and it was because she had so much per-

sonality to put into her **enterprises** and succeeded in putting it into them so completely, that her [farming] affairs **prospered** better than those of her neighbors.

There were certain days in her life, outwardly uneventful, 6 which Alexandra remembered as peculiarly happy; days when she was close to the flat, **fallow** world about her, and felt, as it were, in her own body the joyous **germination** in the soil. There were days, too, which she and Emil had spent together, upon which she loved to look back. There had been such a day when they were down on the river in the dry year, looking over the land. They had made an early start one morning and had driven a long way before noon. When Emil said he was hungry, they drew back from the road . . . and climbed up to the top of a grassy **bluff** to eat their lunch. . . .

The river was clear there, and shallow, since there had been no 7 rain, and it ran in ripples over the sparkling sand. Under the over-hanging willows of the opposite bank there was an inlet where the water was deeper and flowed so slowly that it seemed to sleep in the sun. In this little bay a single wild duck was swimming and diving and **preening** her feathers, **disporting herself** very happily in the **flickering** light and shade.

They sat for a long time, watching the solitary bird take its 8 pleasure. No living thing had ever seemed to Alexandra as beautiful as that wild duck. Emil must have felt about it as she did, for after-ward, when they were at home, he used sometimes to say, "Sister, you know our duck down there—" Alexandra remembered that day as one of the happiest in her life. Years afterward she thought of the duck as still there, swimming and diving all by herself in the sunlight, a kind of **enchanted** bird that did not know age or change.

Most of Alexandra's happy memories were as impersonal as 9 this one; yet to her they were very personal. Her mind was a white book, with clear writing about weather and beasts and growing things. Not many people would have cared to read it; only a happy few. She had never been in love, she had never indulged in senti-mental **reveries**. Even as a girl she had looked upon men as workfel-lows. She had grown up in serious times.

There was one **fancy**, indeed, which persisted through her girl- 10 hood. It most often came to her on Sunday mornings, the one day in the week when she lay abed listening to the familiar morning sounds; the windmill singing in the brisk breeze, Emil whistling as he blacked his boots down by the kitchen door.

Sometimes, as she lay thus luxuriously idle, her eyes closed, 11 she used to have an illusion of being lifted up bodily and carried lightly by someone very strong. It was a man, certainly, who carried her, but he was like no man she knew; he was much larger and stronger and swifter, and he carried her as easily as if she were a **sheaf** of wheat. She never saw him, but, with eyes closed, she could feel that he was yellow like the sunlight, and there was the smell of ripe cornfields about him.

     She could feel him approach, bend over her and lift her, and 12 then she could feel herself being carried swiftly off across the fields. After such a reverie she would rise hastily, angry with herself, and go down to the bath-house that was partitioned off the kitchen shed. There she would stand in a tin tub and **prosecute** her bath with vigor, finishing it by pouring buckets of cold well-water over her gleaming white body which no man on the Divide could have carried very far.

     As she grew older, this fancy more often came to her when 13 she was tired than when she was fresh and strong. Sometimes, after she had been in the open all day, overseeing the **branding** of the cattle or the loading of the pigs, she would come in chilled . . . and go to bed with her body actually **aching** with fatigue. Then, just before she went to sleep, she had the old sensation of being lifted and carried by a strong being who took from her all bodily weariness.

Vocabulary

aching *(adj.)*   suffering pain
bluff *(n.)*   cliff
branding *(n.)*   marking with a hot iron to show ownership
crust *(n.)*   hard surface layer, as of snow
*****disporting herself** *(adj.)*   amusing herself
*****Divide (Continental or Great Divide)** *(n.)*   ridge of the Rocky
    Mountains that separates rivers flowing toward the Atlantic from those
    flowing toward the Pacific
enchanted *(adj.)*   bewitched
enterprise *(n.)*   project; undertaking
exterminate *(v.)*   to destroy entirely
*****fallow** *(adj.)*   dormant; inactive
*****fancy** *(n.)*   mental image
flickering *(adj.)*   wavering; moving unsteadily
germination *(n.)*   beginning of growth
*****hedgerow** *(n.)*   row of bushes enclosing or separating fields

*Denotes low-frequency word.

hue *(n.)* color
perceptible *(adj.)* capable of being observed
***preen** *(v.)* to clean and trim [feathers]
proficient *(adj.)* skilled; adept
***prosecute** *(v.)* to perform
prosper *(v.)* to succeed
recuperate *(v.)* to regain a former state; to recover
reflect *(v.)* to think seriously; to ponder
reverie *(n.)* daydream
***sheaf** *(n.)* stack or bundle, as of corn
shivering *(adv.)* shaking; trembling
***slaty** *(adj.)* gray like slate (a kind of rock)
***stubble** *(n.)* stems of plants remaining in the soil after harvest
***teeming** *(adj.)* abundant
***variegated** *(adj.)* having different colors

Activities

1. Look closely at the text. How does Cather describe the effect of the seasons on the life of the prairie? Make notes in your journal and discuss your ideas with your class.

2. What effect do the seasons have on the people living on the prairie? Compare their feelings with what is happening in nature.

3. Discuss with your class the symbolism of the male figure that Alexandra imagines carries her away. Why do you think she imagines such a figure?

4. Write an essay comparing the effect of winter and spring on the characters in the story.

5. Describe a significant experience you have had with nature. Try to make your audience feel the effect this experience had on you.

For Further Reading

Arnold, Marilyn. *Willa Cather's Short Fiction*. Athens: Ohio UP, 1986.

Randall, John H. *The Landscape and the Looking Glass*. Boston: Houghton, 1960.

Woodress, James. *Willa Cather: A Literary Life*. Lincoln: U of Nebraska P, 1987.

*Denotes low-frequency word.

17

From *Rickshaw*

Lao She (1899–1966)
Fiction: Novel

Background

Fatherless at an early age, Lao She had to work to support himself and his mother. Life was even more difficult because his family were Manchus, members of an ethnic minority from Manchuria in northeast China. Because of their non-Chinese ethnicity, Manchus were called "barbarians" by the ruling majority and were not given equal educational opportunities. Nevertheless, Lao She was an outstanding student who impressed his professors. Eventually he graduated from Beijing Teachers' College as a teacher of Chinese.

In 1924 he went to London, where he taught the Chinese language. During his stay he became familiar with Charles Dickens's nineteenth-century novels about the life of the London poor. It was also during this period that Lao She began to write his own novels, in part because he was so lonely and nostalgic for China. Ultimately Lao She returned to China, where he became a victim of the so-called "Great Cultural Revolution." Like many of China's intellectuals, he received rough treatment by the young revolutionary Red Guards. Directly or indirectly, Lao She's encounter with the Red Guards led to his death in 1966.

The novel *Rickshaw* takes place in 1934, when the Japanese occupied Manchuria, and ends shortly before the outbreak of war between China and Japan. Influenced by the Western Realism of Dickens, Lao She tells the story of a poor country boy, Hsiang Tzu. The orphaned young man has ambitions of leading a better life in the capital city, Beijing. Lao She's sympathetic picture of the tragic struggle of the urban poor in *Rickshaw* has led critics to regard this as his best novel.

Pre-Reading Activities

1. Why do you think people leave rural areas to live in large cities? In a country as densely populated as China, how could a poor person coming from a rural area to a large city make a living?
2. Keeping the issue of overpopulation in mind, what do you think transportation might be like in a large city in a nonindustrialized country? What kinds of vehicles do you think might be used?
3. What do you think an author could do in his writing to show his readers the need for social reform for the poor?

Key Terms

Beijing (formerly Peking)
Chiang Kai-shek (1888–1975)
Cultural Revolution (1966–1976)
Dickens, Charles (1812–1870)
Hsiang Tzu
Manchu/Manchuria
Mao Zedong (1893–1976)

People's Republic of China (Communist)
Puyi
Red Guards
Republic of China (Nationalist)
Taiwan

From *Rickshaw*
Lao She

When Hsiang Tzu rented someone else's rickshaw, he ran from dawn till dark, from east to west, from south to north. He had no say in the matter. He was like a **top** someone else was **spinning**. But in the midst of all this twirling his eyes certainly had no spots before them nor was his mind confused. His thoughts were fixed on that distant rickshaw, the rickshaw that would make him free and independent, the rickshaw that would be like his own hands and feet. He would no longer have to put up with the bad temper of rickshaw agency owners or be hypocritically polite to others when he had his own rickshaw. With his own strength and his own rickshaw, he would have something to eat when he opened his eyes in the morning.

He did not fear hardship and had none of the bad habits of the other rickshaw men, habits which all of them could understand and pardon but were certainly not to be taken as examples of proper be-

Figure 20 • Chinese rickshaw

havior. His intelligence and exertions were enough to realize his ambitions. Had his environment been a little better, had he had a little education, he certainly would not have ended up in the "**rubber tire corps**."

Furthermore, no matter what he worked at, he certainly would never have failed to make the most of his opportunities. Unfortunately, he was compelled to pull a rickshaw. All right, he could prove his ability and intelligence in this occupation, too. He seemed to be just the sort of person who would even be a good **demon** in hell if he had to.   3

Born and reared in a village, he lost both his parents and the few pieces of family land as well. He came to the city when he was eighteen. Bringing with him a country boy's muscles and **forthrightness**, he earned his keep by selling his strength in one day-labor job after another. But he realized before long that pulling a rickshaw was the easiest way of all to earn money. There are limits to the income from other laboring jobs.   4

There was more variety and opportunity in pulling a rickshaw; you never knew when you might gain a reward greater than you had ever hoped for. Naturally he was aware that such an encounter did not come about entirely by chance. It was essential that both man and rickshaw have a handsome air. You can do business with a man who recognizes quality when you have the goods to sell.   5

After thinking it over, he believed that he did have the quali- 6
fications. He was strong and the right age. The trouble was he had
never done the running. He didn't dare just grab hold and take off
with a fine-looking rickshaw. But this was no **insurmountable** difficulty. With his **physique** and strength as a foundation, he would
need only ten or fifteen days of practice to be able to run with style.
Then he would rent a new rickshaw. Perhaps he'd get hired on a private basis very quickly and then, after eating **sparingly** and spending
very little for one year, or two years, or even three or four years, he
would certainly be able to get his own rickshaw, and one of the best!
Looking at his youthful muscles, it seemed to him it was only a question of time until he achieved his ambitions and reached his goal. It
was no dream at all. . . .

He was almost like a tree; **sturdy**, silent, and yet alive. He had 7
his own plans and some insight, but he did not enjoy conversation.
Each man's grievances and difficulties were topics of public discussion among the rickshaw pullers. They all reported, or described, or
yelled about their affairs at the rickshaw stands, in the small tea-
houses, and in front of mixed courtyards, the horizontal **tenements**
of Peking.

Afterwards these tales became everyone's property and like a 8
song were passed along from one place to another. Hsiang Tzu was a
peasant; his speech was not as **glib** as the city fellows'. Assuming that
cleverness of speech comes from **innate** ability, what was innate
with him was an unwillingness to talk. He was also, therefore, not
inclined to copy the **spiteful** lips and wicked tongues of the city folk.
He minded his own business and did not enjoy discussing it with others. Because his mouth was often **idle**, he had plenty of time to
think; his eyes seemed always to be peering at his mind. He needed
only to decide; then he would follow the road his mind had opened.
If it happened that his path was blocked, he would remain silent for
several days, **grinding** his teeth, just as if he were chewing up his
heart.

Vocabulary

corps *(n.)*   group of people under a common direction
   *****"rubber tire corps"** *(n.)*   another name for the rickshaw pullers
demon *(n.)*   devil
forthrightness *(n.)*   directness; frankness

*Denotes low-frequency word.

*glib *(adj.)*   smooth; fluent
*grinding *(adj.)*   pressing together with a turning motion, as when grinding one's teeth
idle *(adj.)*   not active
innate *(adj.)*   natural; inborn (as opposed to acquired)
insurmountable *(adj.)*   incapable of being overcome or conquered
*physique *(n.)*   form of the body
sparingly *(adv.)*   in a very limited way
spin *(v.)*   to cause to rotate quickly
spiteful *(adj.)*   full of evil or meanness
sturdy *(adj.)*   strong
tenement *(n.)*   apartment building (usually not a comfortable one)
*top *(n.)*   a child's toy shaped somewhat like an inverted cone, with a point upon which it is spun, as when released from a string

Activities

1. Working with your study group, make notes in your journal about the background of the main character, Hsiang Tzu. Why do you think the author describes these details? Who is the audience for the novel?
2. What is Hsiang Tzu's personal goal? Given his background, why do you think this goal is important for him?
3. Using your journal notes and what you learned from class, write an essay predicting Hsiang Tzu's future.
4. Write an essay on Lao She's portrayal of Chinese society before the Chinese Revolution. What is his purpose?
5. *Library research:* In an encyclopedia or literary biography, read about the English author Charles Dickens and his work. Write an essay comparing Dickens and Lao She.

For Further Reading

Fairband, John King. *China: A New History.* Cambridge, MA: Harvard UP, 1992.
Meskill, John, et al. *An Introduction to Chinese Civilization.* New York: Columbia UP, 1973.
Spence, Jonathan D. *The Search for Modern China.* New York: Norton, 1990.
Vohra, Ranbir. *Lao She and the Chinese Revolution.* Cambridge, MA: Harvard UP, 1974.

Figure 21A • **Map of precolonial Africa**

18

From *Things Fall Apart*

Chinua Achebe (b. 1925)
Fiction: Novel

Background

Nigerian author Chinua Achebe is an accomplished novelist, short-story writer, poet, and critic. He also has taught and lectured widely in Africa, Europe, and North America. His novel *Things Fall Apart*, first published in England in 1958, is a classic of modern Anglo-African writing and one of the most widely read works by an African.

Africa as a whole and Nigeria in particular are ethnically very diverse. For example, more than 200 languages are spoken in Nigeria. Modern political divisions in Africa were largely determined by imperialist European nations during the Berlin Conference in 1885. These divisions were unrelated to the areas occupied by the various African peoples. As a result, distinct ethnic groups were forced together into one area and conflicts such as the Biafran War (1965–1970) broke out. In this struggle, the Ibo, one of the three main ethnic groups in Nigeria and the group to which Chinua Achebe belonged, tried to become independent. Although they failed, Achebe gained an international reputation speaking out for his people. It is this specific ethnic background that Achebe drew upon for *Things Fall Apart* and the novels that followed it.

Furthermore, *Things Fall Apart* is biographical—that is, Achebe incorporates his own family's history into the book. He describes what Ibo life was like for his grandfather's generation and the "falling apart" of traditional society after British colonial forces arrived in the "Scramble for Africa." The novel describes the precolonial Ibo society and its later conflict with British imperialism by focusing on an important leader, Okonkwo, and his family. Okonkwo's personal tragedy symbolizes the end of traditional Ibo life.

Figure 21B • Map of colonial Africa

Pre-Reading Activities

1. With your study group, review what you know about oral tradition. You may wish to look back at earlier chapters in your book.

2. Chinua Achebe's native language is an African language, Ibo. Why do you think he writes in English?

3. Why do you think Europeans went to Africa in the late nineteenth century? Why do you think they later left?

Key Terms

Berlin Conference (1885)	Nigeria
Biafra; Biafran War (1965–1970)	Nwoye (Okonkwo's son)
colonize/colonization/colonial	Okonkwo
ethnic group	precolonial
Ibo (Igbo)	"Scramble for Africa"
Ikemefuna (Okonkwo's adopted son)	secession
imperialism	Umuofia

From *Things Fall Apart*
Chinua Achebe

For three years Ikemefuna lived in Okonkwo's household and   1
the elders of Umuofia seemed to have forgotten about him. He grew
rapidly like a **yam tendril** in the rainy season, and was full of the
sap of life. He had become wholly absorbed into his new family. He

Figure 22 • **Ibo artisans carving wooden masks** *(Peter Buckley/Photo Researchers)*

was like an elder brother to Nwoye, and from the very first seemed to have **kindled** a new fire in the younger boy. He made him feel grown-up; and they no longer spent the evenings in mother's hut while she cooked, but now sat with Okonkwo in his *obi*, or watched him as he tapped his palm tree for the evening wine. Nothing pleased Nwoye now more than to be sent for by his mother or another of his father's wives to do one of those difficult and masculine tasks in the home, like splitting wood, or **pounding** food. On receiving such a message through a younger brother or sister, Nwoye would **feign** annoyance and **grumble** aloud about women and their troubles.

Okonkwo was inwardly pleased at his son's development, and   2
and he knew it was due to Ikemefuna. He wanted Nwoye to grow into a tough young man capable of ruling his father's household when he was dead and gone to join the ancestors. He wanted him to be a **prosperous** man, having enough in his barn to feed the ancestors with regular sacrifices. And so he was always happy when he heard him grumbling about women. That showed that in time he would be able to control his women-folk. No matter how prosperous a man was, if he was unable to rule his women and his children (and especially his women) he was not really a man. He was like the man in the song who had ten and one wives and not enough soup for his **foo-foo**.

So Okonkwo encouraged the boys to sit with him in his *obi*,   3
and he told them stories of the land—masculine stories of violence and **bloodshed**. Nwoye knew that it was right to be masculine and to be violent, but somehow he still preferred the stories that his mother used to tell, and which she no doubt still told to her younger children—stories of the **tortoise** and his **wily** ways . . . and of the quarrel between Earth and Sky long ago, and how Sky **withheld** rain for seven years, until crops **withered** and the dead could not be buried because the **hoes** broke on the stony Earth. At last **Vulture** was sent to **plead** with Sky, and to soften his heart with a song of the suffering of the sons of men. Whenever Nwoye's mother sang this song he felt carried away to the distant scene in the sky where Vulture, Earth's **emissary**, sang for mercy.

At last Sky was moved to pity, and he gave to Vulture rain   4
wrapped in leaves of coco-yam. But as he flew home his long **talons** pierced the leaves and the rain fell as it had never fallen before. And so heavily did it rain on Vulture that he did not return to deliver his message but flew to a distant land, from where he had espied a fire.

And when he got there he found it was a man making a sacrifice. He warmed himself in the fire and ate the **entrails**.

     That was the kind of story that Nwoye loved. But he now   5 knew that they were for foolish women and children, and he knew that his father wanted him to be a man. And so he feigned that he no longer cared for women's stories. And when he did this he saw that his father was pleased and no longer **rebuked** him or beat him. So Nwoye and Ikemefuna would listen to Okonkwo's stories about tribal wars, or how, years ago, he had stalked his victim, overpowered him, and obtained his first human head.

Vocabulary

bloodshed *(n.)* killing; spilling of human blood
emissary *(n.)* person or agent sent on a specific mission
***entrails** *(n.)* internal organs, especially the intestines
***feign** *(v.)* to pretend
***foo-foo** *(n.)* Ibo food prepared from mashed manioc root
grumble *(v.)* to mutter or complain in an angry manner
***hoe** *(n.)* tool with a thin blade set across the end of a long handle, used for loosening the earth
kindle *(v.)* to light a fire
***obi** *(n.)* Ibo living quarters for the head of the family
plead *(v.)* to beg
pounding *(n.)* beating to a pulp or powder
prosperous *(adj.)* successful; well off
rebuke *(v.)* to criticize sharply
sap *(n.)* any fluid vital to the life of an organism; vigor; energy
***talon** *(n.)* claw of a bird such as a vulture
***tendril** *(n.)* threadlike part of a climbing plant that supports it as it climbs
***tortoise** *(n.)* turtle
***vulture** *(n.)* large bird, related to eagles and hawks, that lives on dead flesh
***wily** *(adj.)* sly; crafty
***wither** *(v.)* to dry up, as from great heat
withhold (withheld) *(v.)* to hold back; to keep back
yam *(n.)* sweet potato having red flesh

* Denotes low-frequency word.

Activities

1. In your study group or alone, make notes in your journal about the roles of men and women in traditional Ibo society as shown in *Things Fall Apart*.

2. Based on your reading, what other values do you believe are important in the Ibo culture? Discuss them with your study group or your class.

3. What evidence of oral tradition do you see in the story? How does the mother's oral tradition differ from the father's?

4. Choose one of the Ibo cultural values discussed above and write an essay explaining why the Ibo would consider this value important.

5. Every novel written by Chinua Achebe is about Nigeria, yet he has chosen to write in English. Since this is the language of the colonial power that controlled Nigeria before 1965, his choice has definite political implications. Write an essay discussing the advantages and disadvantages of writing a nation's literature in the language of a former colonial power.

6. In your study group, try to identify the framed story or story within the story. Discuss the relationship between humans and the gods as portrayed in the framed story. Make notes in your journal.

7. Write an essay comparing the sacrifice to Vulture in *Things Fall Apart* and the sacrifice to Poseidon in *The Odyssey* (Chapter 3).

For Further Reading

Achebe, Chinua. *Hopes and Impediments: Selected Essays.* New York: Doubleday, 1989.

Chinweizu et al. *Toward the Decolonization of African Literature.* Vol. 1. Washington, DC: Howard UP, 1983.

Pakenham, Thomas. *The Scramble for Africa: The White Man's Conquest of the Dark Continent from 1876 to 1912.* New York: Random, 1991.

CHAPTER 19

From *Out of Africa*

Isak Dinesen (1885–1962)
Fiction: Novel

Background

Isak Dinesen is one of the pseudonyms, or pen names, of Baroness Karen Dinesen von Blixen-Finecke, who was born to a wealthy Danish family. As a young woman she emigrated from Denmark to the British colony in Kenya, East Africa, with her fiancé, Baron Bror von Blixen-Finecke. They were part of the emigration that followed the division of Africa by imperialist European governments. The 1890 Anglo-German Treaty divided East Africa into English and German colonies where European settlers were encouraged to set up businesses, plantations, and mines.

The Blixens purchased a farm on which they tried to grow coffee. Seventeen years later, both the farm and the marriage were in ruins. Suffering physically and psychologically, Isak Dinesen returned to her family in Denmark at age 46. It was through her writing that she managed to survive this painful experience.

The publication of her collection of stories, *Seven Gothic Tales* (1934), established her as one of the most significant European women writers of the mid-1930s. The earliest versions of these stories were begun in Africa. Her next work, *Out of Africa* (1937), has been considered an important landmark in colonial literature. A Romantic memoir of Dinesen's years in Africa, it was conceived and written after her return to Denmark. Like Wordsworth, she recreates the African landscape in recollection, focusing on her sensations and impressions. Her views of the African ethnic groups she encountered, especially the Kikuyu and the Muslim Somali, are Eurocentric—that is, colored by a European perspective.

With the publication of *Out of Africa*, Dinesen made her name as a modern classical writer. Further African reminiscences followed with *Shadows on the Grass* (1961). In 1985 the award-winning film *Out of Africa* was released, resulting in a renewed interest in the life and works of Isak Dinesen.

Pre-Reading Activities

1. With your study group or class, discuss what you think might be the attitudes of a colonial power toward the people of its colonies.
2. Romantic (nineteenth-century) European writers are interested in exotic places. What might they focus on when writing about Africa?

Key Terms

Anglo-German Treaty (1890)   Muslim
colonial literature   nostalgia
East Africa   pseudonym
Eurocentric view   simile
Kenya   Somali
Kikuyu   Swaheli

From *Out of Africa*
Isak Dinesen

I had a farm in Africa, at the foot of the Ngong Hills. The Equa-   1
tor runs across these highlands, a hundred miles to the North, and the farm lay at an altitude of over six thousand feet. In the day-time you felt that you had got high up, near to the sun, but the early mornings and evenings were **limpid** and restful, and the nights were cold.

The geographical position and the height of the land combined   2
to create a landscape that [was not like anything] in all the world. There was no fat on it and no **luxuriance** anywhere; it was Africa **distilled** up through six thousand feet, like the strong and refined **essence** of a continent. The colors were dry and burnt, like the colors in pottery. The trees had a light delicate foliage, the structure of which was different from that of the trees in Europe; it did not grow in **bows** or **cupolas**, but in horizontal layers, and the formation gave

to the tall solitary trees a likeness to the palms, or a heroic and romantic air like **fullrigged** ships with their sails **clewed up**, and to the edge of a wood a strange appearance as if the whole wood were faintly **vibrating**. Upon the grass of the great plains the crooked bare old thorn-trees were scattered, and the grass was spiced like **thyme** and **bogmyrtle**; in some places the scent was so strong, that it **smarted** in the nostrils. . . . The views were immensely wide. Everything that you saw made for greatness and freedom, and unequalled nobility.

The chief feature of the landscape, and of your life in it, was   3 the air. Looking back on a **sojourn** in the African highlands, you are struck by your feeling of having lived for a time up in the air. The sky was rarely more than pale blue or violet, with a **profusion** of mighty, weightless, ever-changing clouds towering up and sailing on it, but it has a blue **vigor** in it, and at a short distance it painted the ranges of hills and the woods a fresh deep blue. In the middle of the day the air was alive over the land, like a flame burning; it **scintillated**, waved and shone like running water, mirrored and doubled all objects, and created great **Fata Morgana**. Up in this high air you breathed easily, drawing in a vital assurance and lightness of heart. In the highlands you woke up in the morning and thought: Here I am, where I ought to be. . . .

I had six thousand acres of land, and had thus got much spare   4 land besides the coffee-plantation. Part of the farm was native forest, and about one thousand acres were squatters' land, what [the Kikuyu] called their *shambas*. The squatters are Natives, who with their families hold a few acres on a white man's farm, and in return have to work for him a certain number of days in the year. My squatters, I think, saw the relationship in a different light, for many of them were born on the farm, and their fathers before them, and they very likely regarded me as a sort of superior squatter on their estates. The squatters' land was more intensely alive than the rest of the farm, and was changing with the seasons the year round. The **maize** grew up higher than your head as you walked on the narrow **hard-trampled** footpaths in between the tall green rustling **regiments**. . . . The beans ripened in the fields, were gathered and **thrashed** by the women, and the stalks and pods were collected and burned, so that in certain seasons thin blue columns of smoke rose here and there all over the farm. The Kikuyu also grew the sweet potatoes, that have a vinelike leaf and spread over the ground like a dense **entangled** mat, and many varieties of big yellow and green **speckled** pumpkins. . . .

Nairobi was our town, twelve miles away. . . . Here were the   5
Government House and the big central offices; from here the country
was ruled. . . . The quarters of the Natives and of the colored immi-
grants were very extensive compared to the European town.

The Swaheli town . . . had not a good name in any way, but   6
was a lively, dirty and **gaudy** place, with, at any hour, a number of
things going on in it. It was built mostly out of old paraffin tins hammered flat, in various states of rust, like the coral rock, the fossilized
structure, from which the spirit of the advancing civilization was
steadily fleeing.

The Somali town was farther away from Nairobi, on account,   7
I think, of the Somalis' system of **seclusion** of their women. There
were in my day a few beautiful young Somali women, of whom all
the town knew the names, who went and lived in the Bazaar and led
the Nairobi Police a great dance; they were intelligent, and **bewitching** people. But the honest Somali women were not seen in the
town. The Somali town lay exposed to all winds and was shadeless
and dusty, it must have recalled to the Somali their native deserts.

Europeans, who live for a long time, even for several genera-   8
tions, in the same place, cannot **reconcile themselves** to the
complete indifference to the surroundings of their homes, of the **nomadic** races. The Somalis' houses were irregularly **strewn** on the
bare ground, and looked as if they had been nailed together with a
bushel of four-inch nails, to last for a week. It was a surprising thing,
when you entered one of them, to find it inside so neat and fresh,
scented with Arab incenses, with fine carpets and hangings, **vessels**
of brass and silver, and swords with ivory **hilts** and noble blades.

The Somali women themselves had dignified, gentle ways, and   9
were hospitable and gay, with a laughter like silver bells. I was much
at home in the Somali village through my Somali servant Farah
Aden, who was with me all the time that I was in Africa, and I went
to many of their feasts. A big Somali wedding is a magnificent, traditional festivity. As a guest of honor I was taken into the bridal chamber, where the walls and bridal bed were hung with old gently glow-
ing weavings and **embroideries**, and the dark-eyed young bride
herself was stiff, like a **marshal's baton** with heavy silks, gold and
amber.

The Somali were cattle-dealers and traders all over the coun-   10
try. For the transport of their **goods** they kept a number of little grey
donkeys in the village, and I have seen camels there as well:
haughty, hardened products of the desert, beyond all earthly sufferings, like Cactus, and like the Somali.

Vocabulary

bewitching *(adj.)* attractive as if by the power of witchcraft

***bogmyrtle** *(n.)* fragrant plant that grows in wet, spongy ground

bow *(n.)* something bent into a simple curve; arch

***clewed up** *(adj.)* rolled or hauled up

***cupola** *(n.)* arched structure resting on a circular base forming a covering

distilled *(adj.)* concentrated

***embroidery** *(n.)* needlework done with thread on cloth

entangled *(adj.)* twisted together

essence *(n.)* real or ultimate nature of a thing

***Fata Morgana** *(n.)* mirage; illusion

***fullrigged** *(adj.)* having the maximum number of sails and masts (used in describing a ship)

gaudy *(adj.)* flashy; tastelessly ornamented

goods *(n. pl.)* wares; merchandise

***hard-trampled** *(adj.)* heavily walked on

haughty *(adj.)* scornfully proud

***hilt** *(n.)* handle of a sword

limpid *(adj.)* clear

***luxuriance** *(n.)* lushness

***maize** *(n.)* corn

***marshal's baton** *(n.)* slender stick carried by a high military officer as a symbol of office

nomadic *(adj.)* wandering from place to place, usually seasonally in order to get food

profusion *(n.)* great quantity

reconcile oneself *(v.)* to make oneself accept

regiment *(n.)* ordered rows, usually military

scintillate *(v.)* to sparkle

seclusion *(n.)* isolation; removal from outside influence

***smart** *(v.)* to cause sharp pain

sojourn *(n.)* temporary stay

***speckled** *(adj.)* spotted

***strew (strewed, strewn)** *(v.)* to scatter

***thrash** *(v.)* to separate the seeds from the rest of a plant

***thyme** *(n.)* plant of the mint family with fragrant leaves

vessel *(n.)* container such as a cup, bowl, or kettle

vibrate *(v.)* to move back and forth quickly; to quiver

vigor *(n.)* force

*Denotes low-frequency word.

Activities

1. Dinesen refers many times to nature in her story. Read the story closely, making notes in your journal of the images she uses to describe nature. Discuss your notes with your group.

2. Based on your notes and discussion, write a summary of the way Isak Dinesen presents nature in her story.

3. What is Dinesen's attitude toward the native Africans in the story? Does she portray the Somali and the Kikuyu in the same way?

4. In an essay, compare life in Africa as shown in *Things Fall Apart* (Chapter 18) with how it is shown in *Out of Africa*. Why are the two depictions different?

For Further Reading

Johannesson, Eric O. *The World of Isak Dinesen.* Seattle: U of Washington P, 1961.

Langbaum, Robert. *The Gayety of Vision: A Study of Isak Dinesen's Art.* New York: Random, 1964.

Thurman, Judith. *Isak Dinesen, The Life of a Storyteller.* New York: St. Martin's, 1982.

Trzebinski, Errol. *Silence Will Speak: Denys Finch Hatton and Karen Blixen.* Chicago: U of Chicago P, 1977.

20

From *The Woman in the Dunes*

Kobo Abe (1924–1993)
Fiction: Philosophical Novel

Background

Perhaps Kobo Abe's early sense of alienation derived from his growing up in Japanese-occupied Manchuria, China, outside of his native Japan. As a young man, he entertained his classmates by reciting the Gothic tales of the American writer Edgar Allan Poe. Like the male protagonist of *The Woman in the Dunes*, he also enjoyed doing mathematical puzzles and collecting insects.

After returning to Tokyo, Japan, he developed tuberculosis and during his hospitalization devoured the works of the Russian Existentialist novelist Fyodor Dostoevsky. As Japan became more deeply involved in World War II, Abe felt a further sense of alienation from his culture and continued to read the work of Western philosophers such as Nietzsche, Jaspers, and Heidegger, and of the Existentialist author Franz Kafka.

The end of the war found Abe again in Manchuria, where his father died during a typhus epidemic. Although suffering poverty and ill health, Abe studied to become a medical doctor like his father and graduated in 1948. But he soon decided to undertake a career as a writer.

Like many intellectuals in the 1950s, Abe was shocked at the destructive horror of the dropping of two atomic bombs on Japan in order to end World War II. The cost of the war was tremendous, not only in human lives but in the devastation of traditional Japanese life. In an interview in the 1960s, Abe stated, "I will never forget that my adolescence began amidst death and ruin."

The Woman in the Dunes is a strange story that shows strong Western philosophical influence. Neither of the important characters—the man and the woman—has a personal name in the story.

Pre-Reading Activities

1. With your study group, discuss your feelings about the meaning of life. Do you think your ideas are different from your parents' or grandparents' ideas? In what way are they different (or the same)?
2. Do you believe that science and technology make our lives better than our grandparents' lives were? Are any of the changes made by technology causing our lives to be worse? How?

Key Terms

Camus, Albert (1913–1960)   Manchuria
cross-cultural influence   metamorphosis
dehumanization   philosophy/philosophical novel
Dostoevsky, Fyodor (1821–1881)   Sartre, Jean-Paul (1905–1980)
Existentialism/Existentialist

From *The Woman in the Dunes*
Kobo Abe

When he had finished carrying the kerosene cans over the   1
second time, he heard the sound of voices, and on the road above a
hand lamp **flickered**.

The woman spoke rather sharply. "It's the lift basket. I've al-   2
ready finished over here. Give me some help over there, will you?"

For the first time he **grasped** the meaning of the sandbags   3
that lay buried at the top of the ladder: by running the ropes around
them, the baskets could be raised and lowered. Four men managed
each basket, and there were two or three groups in all. For the most
part, they appeared to be young men who worked briskly and effi-
ciently. By the time the basket of one group was full, the next group
was already waiting to take over. In six hauls, the sand which had
been piled up was completely leveled off.

"Those fellows are amazing!"   4

His tone was friendly as he wiped away the sweat with his   5 shirt sleeve. The young men, who **uttered** not a word of ridicule at his helping with the sand, appeared to devote themselves energetically to their work. He felt **well-disposed** toward them.

"Yes. In our village we really follow the motto 'Love Your Home'." 6

"What sort of love is that?" 7

"It's the love you have for where you live." 8

"Great!" 9

He laughed, and she laughed with him. But she did not seem 10 to understand the reason for her laughter herself.

From afar came the sound of a three-wheeled truck starting 11 up.

"Well now, shall we take a rest?" [he said]. 12

"Oh no. When they finish with one round they come right 13 back again with the basket."

"Oh, let it go. The rest can wait until tomorrow and . . ." 14

He arose unconcerned and began walking toward the 15 earthen floor, but she showed no signs of coming along with him.

"You can't do things that way! We've got to work at least once 16 all around the house."

"What do you mean, 'all around'?" 17

"Well, we can't let the house be smashed, can we? The sand 18 comes down from all sides."

"But it'll take until morning to do that." 19

As though challenged, she turned abruptly and hurried off. 20 She apparently intended to return to the base of the cliff and continue her work. Quite like the behavior of the **beetle**, he thought.

Now that he understood this, he certainly wouldn't be taken 21 in again.

"I'm **dumbfounded**! Is it like this every night?" 22

"The sand never stops. The baskets and the three-wheeler keep 23 going the whole night through."

"I suppose they do." And indeed they did. The sand never 24 stopped falling. The man was completely at a loss. He was bewildered, rather as if he had casually stepped on the tail of a snake that he had thought to be small but had turned out to be surprisingly large; by the time he had realized this, its head was already threatening him from behind.

"But this means you exist only for the purpose of clearing 25 away the sand, doesn't it?"

"Yes, but we just can't sneak away at night, you know." 26

He was more and more upset. He had no intention of becoming involved in such a life. 27

"Yes, you can. It would be simple, wouldn't it? You can do   28
anything if you want to."

"No, that wouldn't be right at all." She spoke casually, breath-   29
ing in rhythm with her shoveling. "The village keeps going because
we never let up clearing away the sand like this. If we stopped, in ten
days the village would be completely buried. Next it will be the
neighbor's turn in back. See, there."

"Very praiseworthy, I'm sure. And do the basket gangs work so   30
hard for the same reason?"

"Well, they do get some pay from the town."   31

"If they have that much money, why don't they build a more   32
permanent hedge of trees against the sand?"

"It seems to be cheaper to do it this way . . . when you fig-   33
ure the costs."

"This way? Is this really a way?" Suddenly a feeling of anger   34
welled up in him. He was angry at the things that bound the woman
. . . and at the woman who let herself be bound. "Why must you
cling so to such a village? I really don't understand. This sand is not a
trifling matter. You're greatly mistaken if you think you can set
yourself up against it with such methods. It's preposterous! Absurd! I
give up. I really give up. I have absolutely no sympathy for you."

Tossing the shovel on the kerosene cans which had been left   35
out, he abruptly returned to the room, ignoring the expression on
the woman's face.

He spent a sleepless night, turning and tossing. He **pricked up**   36
his ears, sensing the woman's presence. He felt somewhat guilty.
Taking such a stand in front of her was actually an expression of jealousy at what **bound** her; and was it not also a desire that she should
put aside her work and come secretly to his bed? Actually, his strong
feelings were apparently not simply anger at female stupidity. There
was something more **unfathomable**.

[Although he had laughed at her unscientific observation that   37
sand absorbed water, now he saw that] his mattress was getting
damper and damper, and the sand more and more **clammy** to his
skin. It was all too unreasonable, too **eerie**.

There was no need to blame himself for having thrown the   38
shovel aside and come in. He did not have to take that much respon-
sibility. Besides, the obligations he had to assume were already more
than enough. In fact, his involvement with the sand and his insect
collecting were, after all, simply ways to escape, however temporar-
ily, from his obligations and the inactivity of his life.

No matter how he tried, he could not sleep.   39

Vocabulary

*beetle *(n.)*   insect with hard outer wings
bind (bound, bound) *(v.)*   to hold; to restrain
*clammy *(adj.)*   damp; moist; sticky
dumbfounded *(adj.)*   astonished; amazed
eerie *(adj.)*   frightening because of strangeness
flicker *(v.)*   to burn or shine unsteadily
grasp *(v.)*   to understand
*prick up one's ears *(v. phrase)*   to listen intensely
*trifling *(adj.)*   unimportant
unfathomable *(adj.)*   not understandable
utter *(v.)*   to speak
well-disposed *(adj.)*   positive; favorable

Activities

1.   Read aloud the dialogue between the woman and the man. Have a narrator read the man's inner thoughts.
2.   The protagonist is a science teacher who tries to find a rational explanation for everything. Alone or with a partner, make a note of passages from the text that show him using his reason.
3.   Look again at the text; make a note of passages where the scientist's reason does *not* explain what is happening. What do you think is the author's purpose in showing this?
4.   Notice that the two characters have no personal names, but are "the man" and "the woman." In what way is this symbolic?
5.   Write an essay contrasting the man's existentialist view of life with the simple view of the woman in the dunes.
6.   Write an essay on the limits of reason in this selection from Kobo Abe's novel *The Woman in the Dunes.*

For Further Reading

Barnes, Hazel. *The Literature of Possibility; A Study of Humanistic Existentialism.* Lincoln: U of Nebraska P, 1959.
Currie, William. *Abe Kobo's Nightmare World of Sand.* New York: Knopf, 1976.
Hibbett, Howard, ed. *Contemporary Japanese Literature.* New York: Knopf, 1983.

*Denotes low-frequency word.

21

From *Chronicle of a Death Foretold*

Gabriel García Márquez (b. 1928)
Fiction: Novella

Background

In the first half of the twentieth century, the fiction of Latin America largely mirrored various regional and national customs. However, the 1940s saw the translation into Spanish of important international authors such as Proust, Joyce, Woolf, and Faulkner. As a result, that decade saw the appearance of several Central and South American writers, such as Guatemalan Miguel Angel Asturias, who took the novel in new directions.

The next generation of Latin American novelists brought a new and important feature to their Modernist work: the role of the imaginative world. Mimesis, or the imitation of reality, was replaced with invention. By the 1960s, the creativity and brilliance of Latin American novelists had produced a so-called "boom" that was internationally recognized. Works coming out of this period, characterized by the fantastic and inventive reality called Magical Realism, included Julio Cortazar's *Hopscotch* (1963) and Manuel Puig's 1968 work, *Betrayed by Rita Hayworth*. It was in this prolific period that Gabriel García Márquez began to write.

García Márquez was born in the small village of Aracataca in Colombia, South America. From his grandparents he heard the local oral tradition and myths. García Márquez recreated this tiny, forgotten inland port of call in his fictional and mythological village, Macondo, which appears in many of his works. García Márquez studied law after graduating from high school but soon became an international journalist for a Colombian newspaper.

García Márquez spent some years living and visiting abroad, and, after the Cuban Revolution in 1959, joined Prensa Latina, a Cuban news agency, first in Bogotá, Colombia, and then in New York. His left-wing political views have been widely publicized, making him unwelcome in anti-Communist circles. Since 1975 he has lived mostly in Mexico, where he continues to write. His most famous novel, *One Hundred Years of Solitude*, was published in 1967 and took the international literary world by storm. It has been translated from Spanish into more than 30 languages. For his years of consistently outstanding literary production, García Márquez was awarded the Nobel Prize in literature in 1982.

In his novella *Chronicle of a Death Foretold*, García Márquez tells of the murder of an innocent young man, Santiago Nasar, in a small Colombian village. The end of the story is told first. Then the details are recreated by an unnamed omniscient narrator through the recollections of a number of the villagers; as each person tells his or her story, the same moments are relived over and over but are seen from a different perspective. Thus the story compresses time and does not follow normal chronological order.

García Márquez uses a stream of consciousness to reveal his characters in a state of stagnation, decay, and solitude. The close reader will also note the religious symbolism in the names of the story's characters and their parallels with the New Testament story of Christ.

Pre-Reading Activities

1. With your study group, discuss what you believe is the role of a man's honor in traditional family life. What is the role of a woman's honor?

2. How do you think someone who is accused of a crime should be treated? Discuss your ideas with your group or class.

Key Terms

Colombia   omniscient narrator
Latin American "boom" of the 1960s   perspective
Magical Realism   South America
Modernist   stream of consciousness
Nobel Prize in Literature   symbolism

Figure 23 • **Modern Central American village with church** *(Carole M. Shaffer-Koros)*

From *Chronicle of a Death Foretold*
Gabriel García Márquez

On the day they were going to kill him, Santiago Nasar got up   1
at five-thirty in the morning to wait for the boat the **bishop** was
coming on. . . .

[Santiago Nasar] had slept little and poorly, without getting   2
undressed, and he woke up with a headache and a **sediment** of cop-
per stirrup on his palate, and he interpreted them as the natural
havoc of the wedding **revels** that had gone on until after midnight.
Furthermore: all the many people he ran into after leaving his house
at five minutes past six and until he was carved up like a pig an hour
later remembered him as being a little sleepy but in a good mood,
and he remarked to all of them in a casual way that it was a very
beautiful day. No one was certain if he was referring to the state of
the weather.

Many people **coincided** in recalling that it was a radiant   3
morning with a sea breeze coming in through the banana groves, as

was to be expected in a fine February of that period. But most agreed that the weather was **funereal**, with a cloudy, low sky and the thick smell of still waters, and that at the moment of the misfortune a thin **drizzle** was falling like . . . one Santiago Nasar had seen in his dream. . . . I was recovering from the wedding revels in the **apostolic** lap of Maria Alejandrina Cervantes, and I only awakened with the **clamor** of the alarm bells, thinking they had turned them loose in honor of the bishop. . . .

I saw [Santiago] in [his mother's] memory. He had just turned   4
twenty-one the last week in January, and he was slim and pale and had his father's Arab eyelids and curly hair. He was the only child of a **marriage of convenience** without a single moment of happiness. . . . From her he had inherited a sixth sense. From his father he learned at a very early age the manipulation of **firearms**, his love for horses, and the mastery of high-flying birds of prey, but from him he also learned the good arts of **valor** and **prudence**. They spoke Arabic between themselves, but not in front of [his mother] Placida Linero, so that she wouldn't feel **excluded**.

They were never seen armed in town, and the only time they   5
brought in their trained birds was for a demonstration of **falconry** at a charity bazaar. The death of his father had forced him to abandon his studies at the end of secondary school in order to take charge of the family ranch. By his nature, Santiago Nasar was merry and peaceful, and openhearted. . . .

It had struck six and the street lights were still on. In the   6
branches of the almond trees and on some balconies the colored wedding decorations were still hanging and one might have thought they'd just been hung in honor of the bishop. . . . When Santiago Nasar left his house, several people were running toward the docks, **hastened** along by the **bellowing** of the boat.

The only place open on the square was a milk shop on one   7
side of the church, where the two men were who were waiting for Santiago Nasar in order to kill him. . . . They were twins: Pedro and Pablo Vicario. They were twenty-four years old, and they looked so much alike that it was difficult to tell them apart. "They were hard-looking, but of a good sort," the report said. I, who had known them since grammar school, would have written the same thing. That morning they were still wearing their dark wedding suits, too heavy and formal for the Caribbean, and they looked **devastated** by so many hours of bad living, but they'd done their duty and shaved. . . .

Angela Vicario was the youngest daughter of a family of **scant**   8
resources. Her father, Poncio Vicario, was a poor man's goldsmith,

and he'd lost his sight from doing so much fine work in gold in order to maintain the honor of the house. Purisima del Carmen, her mother, had been a schoolteacher until she married for ever. Her **meek** and somewhat **afflicted** look hid the strength of her character quite well. "She looked like a **nun**," my wife Mercedes recalls. She devoted herself with such spirit of sacrifice to the care of her husband and the rearing of her children that at times one forgot that she still existed. . . . The brothers were brought up to be men. The girls had been reared to get married. . . .

"Any man will be happy with them because they've been raised to suffer," [my mother said]. . . . No one would have thought, nor did anyone say, that Angela Vicario wasn't a virgin. She hadn't known any previous fiancé and she'd grown up along with her sisters under the **rigor** of a mother of iron. Even when it was less than two months before she would be married, Pura Vicario wouldn't let her go alone with [her husband-to-be] Bayardo San Roman to see the house where they were going to live, but she and the blind father accompanied her to watch over her honor. . . .

[On the wedding night] Pura Vicario had fallen into a deep sleep, when there was knocking on the door. "They were three very slow knocks," she told my mother, "but they had that strange touch of bad news about them." . . . [She] saw Bayardo San Roman in the glow of the street light, his silk shirt unbuttoned and his fancy pants held up by elastic suspenders. "He had that green color of dreams," Pura Vicario told my mother. Angela Vicario was in the shadows. . . . Her satin dress was in **shreds** and she was wrapped in a towel up to the waist. Pura Vicario thought they'd gone off the road in the car. . . .

"Holy Mother of God," she said in terror. "Answer me if you're still of this world."

Bayardo San Roman didn't enter, but softly pushed his wife into the house without speaking a word. Then he kissed Pura Vicario on the cheek and spoke to her in a very deep, **dejected** voice, but with great tenderness. "Thank you for everything, Mother," he told her. "You're a saint."

. . . The twins returned home a short time before three, urgently summoned by their mother. . . . Pedro Vicario, the more forceful of the brothers, picked [Angela] up by the waist and sat her on the dining room table.

"All right, girl," he said to her, **trembling** with rage, "tell us who it was."

She took the time necessary to say the name. She looked for

it in the shadows, she found it at first sight among the many, many easily confused names from this world and the other, and she nailed it to the wall with her well-aimed **dart**, like a butterfly with no will whose sentence has always been written.

"Santiago Nasar," she said.   16

Vocabulary

afflicted *(adj.)*   troubled; distressed

*apostolic *(adj.)*   relating to an apostle (one sent on a mission), especially any of the 12 apostles of Christ

*bellowing *(n.)*   loud, deep, hollow sound characteristic of a bull

bishop *(n.)*   member of the Christian clergy who supervises other clergy, typically governing a diocese

clamor *(n.)*   loud, continuous noise

coincide *(v.)*   to be in agreement; to concur

dart *(n.)*   small missile, usually with a pointed tip at one end and feathers at the other

dejected *(adj.)*   disheartened; discouraged

devastated *(adj.)*   overwhelmed; overcome

drizzle *(n.)*   fine, misty rain

excluded *(adj.)*   barred from participation or inclusion

*falconry *(n.)*   art and sport of training hawks to hunt in cooperation with a person

firearm *(n.)*   weapon from which a shot is fired by gunpowder

*funereal *(adj.)*   suggesting a funeral or burial

hastened *(adj.)*   hurried

havoc *(n.)*   confusion; disorder

*marriage of convenience *(n.)*   marriage contracted for social, political, or economic advantage rather than for mutual affection

meek *(adj.)*   submissive

nun *(n.)*   woman belonging to a religious order, especially one under the vows of poverty, chastity, and obedience

prudence *(n.)*   ability to exercise sound judgment in practical matters

*revel *(n.)*   wild party or celebration

rigor *(n.)*   strictness

scant *(adj.)*   barely sufficient

*sediment *(n.)*   deposited material

shred *(n.)*   long, narrow strip cut or torn off

trembling *(adj.)*   shaking involuntarily; shivering

valor *(n.)*   personal bravery

*Denotes low-frequency word.

Activities

1. Magical Realism combines reality with fantastic, inventive events. Look closely at the text. Alone or with a partner, make notes about important events that seem realistic and those that are fantastic.
2. Look closely at the text. Who is telling the story? What do we know about the narrator?
3. What is the crime of which Santiago Nasar is accused? What is his punishment? Who punishes him? Write an essay agreeing or disagreeing with the punishment.
4. In your journal, make notes on the roles of both women and men in García Márquez's story. In an essay, analyze the roles of men and women in the story.
5. Write an essay on the treatment of honor in *Chronicle of a Death Foretold*.
6. Write an essay on Magical Realism in *Chronicle of a Death Foretold*.

For Further Reading

Byk, John. "From Fact to Fiction: Gabriel García Márquez and the Short Story." *Mid-American Review* 6 (1986): 111–16.

McMurray, George, ed. *Critical Essays on Gabriel García Márquez*. Boston: Houghton, 1987.

Williams, Raymond L. *Gabriel García Márquez*. Boston: Twayne, 1984.

CHAPTER 22

From "Boys and Girls"

Alice Munro (b. 1931)
Fiction: Short Story

Background

Alice Munro was born Alice Laidlaw to a family of Scots descent in Ontario, Canada. Her father, Robert Laidlaw, became a breeder of silver foxes shortly before he married Anne Chamney, a schoolteacher. Their daughter Alice spent her youth in small-town Wingham and from 1949 to 1951 attended the University of Western Ontario, where she majored in English and began to write. In 1951 Alice married James Munro; she spent the next 20 years living on the west coast of Canada, where their three daughters were born. In 1971 she returned to Ontario to be close to her father and her former home. Following a second marriage, she moved to her present home in Clinton, Ontario.

Munro is widely recognized as a major North American author and has won several Canadian Governor-General's Awards for her outstanding fiction. "Boys and Girls" is from her first collection, *Dance of the Happy Shades*, which appeared in Canada in 1968 and was dedicated to her father. In this early story, the conflict between mother and daughter is readily apparent.

Pre-Reading Activities

1. With your study group or class, discuss ways in which adults treat girls and boys differently. Why do you think they do this?
2. How do you think family life on a farm is different from life in the city? Discuss your ideas with your class.

Key Terms

autobiographical	provincial
feminist	Realism
gender role	rural
Ontario, Canada	sexist
postmodern	

From "Boys and Girls"
Alice Munro

My father was a fox farmer. That is, he raised **silver foxes**, in 1
pens; and in the fall and early winter, when their fur was **prime**, he
killed them and skinned them and sold their pelts to the Hudson's
Bay Company or the Montreal Fur Traders. These companies sup-
plied us with heroic calendars to hang, one on each side of the
kitchen door. . . .

[M]y father worked after supper in the cellar of our house. The 2
cellar was **white-washed**, and lit by several hundred-watt bulbs
over the worktable. My brother Laird and I sat on the top step and
watched. My father removed the pelt inside-out from the body of the
fox, which looked surprisingly small, mean and ratlike, **deprived** of
its arrogant weight of fur.

The naked, slippery bodies were collected in a **sack** and buried 3
at the **dump**. One time the hired man, Henry Bailey, had taken a
swipe at me with this sack, saying, "Christmas present!" My mother
thought that was not funny. In fact she disliked the whole pelting operation—that was what the killing, skinning, and preparation of the
furs was called—and wished it did not have to take place in the
house. . . .

Alive, the foxes inhabited a world my father made for them. 4
It was surrounded by a high guard fence, like a medieval town, with
a gate that was **padlocked** at night. Along the streets of this town
were ranged large, sturdy pens. . . . Everything was tidy and **ingenious**; my father was tirelessly inventive and his favorite book in the
world was *Robinson Crusoe*. He had fitted a tin **drum** on a **wheelbarrow**, for bringing water down to the pens. This was my job in
summer, when the foxes had to have water twice a day. . . .

Besides carrying water I helped my father when he cut the 5
long grass. . . . He cut with the **scythe** and I **raked** into piles. Then

he took a **pitchfork** and threw fresh-cut grass all over the tops of the pens, to keep the foxes cooler and shade their coats. . . . My father did not talk to me unless it was about the job we were doing.

In this he was quite different from my mother, who, if she was feeling cheerful, would tell me all sorts of things—the name of a dog she had had when she was a little girl, the names of boys she had gone out with later on when she was grown up, and what certain dresses of hers had looked like—she could not imagine now what had become of them.   6

Whatever thoughts and stories my father had were private, and I was shy of him and would never ask him questions. Nevertheless I worked willingly under his eyes, and with a feeling of pride. One time a **feed** salesman came down into the pens to talk to him and my father said, "Like to have you meet my new hired man." I turned away and raked furiously, red in the face with pleasure.   7

"Could [have] fooled me," said the salesman. "I thought it was only a girl."   8

. . . I hated the hot dark kitchen in summer, the green **blinds** and the **flypapers**, the same old oilcloth table and wavy mirror and bumpy **linoleum**. My mother was too tired and **preoccupied** to talk to me, she had no heart to tell about the Normal School Graduation Dance; sweat **trickled** over her face and she was always counting under her breath, pointing at jars, **dumping** cups of sugar. It seemed to me that work in the house was endless, dreary and peculiarly depressing; work done out of doors, and in my father's service, was **ritualistically** important.   9

I **wheeled** the tank up to the barn, where it was kept, and I heard my mother saying, "Wait till Laird gets a little bigger, then you'll have a real help."   10

What my father said I did not hear. I was pleased by the way he stood listening, politely as he would to a salesman or a stranger, but with an **air** of wanting to get on with his real work. I felt my mother had no business down here and I wanted him to feel the same way. What did she mean about Laird? He was no help to anybody. Where was he now? Swinging himself sick on the swing, going around in circles, or trying to catch **caterpillars**. He never once stayed with me till I was finished.   11

"And then I can use her more in the house," I heard my mother say. She had a dead-quiet, **regretful** way of talking about me that always made me uneasy. "I just get my back turned and she runs off. It's not like I had a girl in the family at all."   12

I went and sat on a feed bag in the corner of the barn, not   13 wanting to appear when this conversation was going on. My mother, I felt, was not to be trusted. She was kinder than my father and more easily fooled, but you could not depend on her, and the real reasons for the things she said and did were not to be known. She loved me, and she sat up late at night making a dress of the difficult style I wanted, for me to wear when school started, but she was also my enemy.

She was always **plotting**. She was plotting now to get me to   14
stay in the house more, although she knew I hated it (*because* she knew I hated it) and keep me from working for my father. It seemed to me she would do this simply out of **perversity**, and to try her power. It did not occur to me that she could be lonely, or jealous. No grown-up could be; they were too fortunate. I sat and kicked my heels **monotonously** against a feedbag, raising dust, and did not come out till she was gone.

At any rate, I did not expect my father to pay any attention to   15
what she said. Who could imagine Laird doing my work—Laird remembering the padlock and cleaning out the watering-dishes with a leaf on the end of a stick, or even wheeling the tank without it tumbling over? It showed how little my mother knew about the way things really were.

Vocabulary

air *(n.)*   look; appearance
blind *(n.)*   window shade
***caterpillar** *(n.)*   wormlike larva of a butterfly or moth
deprived *(adj.)*   marked by loss
***drum** *(n.)*   container in the shape of a cylinder
dump *(n.)*   place where garbage is brought
dump *(v.)*   to throw down
***feed** *(n.)*   food for farm animals
***flypaper** *(n.)*   sticky paper that catches flies
ingenious *(adj.)*   clever
***linoleum** *(n.)*   kind of floor covering
monotonously *(adv.)*   without varying or changing
padlock *(n.)*   lock with a particular kind of lock
pen *(n.)*   enclosed space for animals
perversity *(n.)*   stubborn contrariness; obstinacy
***pitchfork** *(n.)*   long-handled fork for use in farm work
plot *(v.)*   to plan secretly; to scheme

*Denotes low-frequency word.

preoccupied *(adj.)*   lost in thought; absorbed mentally in some other matter

prime *(adj.)*   of the highest quality

rake *(v.)*   to gather together using a rake (a tool with a long handle and short prongs)

regretful *(adj.)*   sorrowful; remorseful

*ritualistically *(adv.)*   ceremonially

*Robinson Crusoe *(n.)*   the name of a book written by Daniel Defoe in 1719; also the name of its hero. Crusoe, an English sailor, managed to live for years by making clever inventions after being shipwrecked on a tropical island.

sack *(n.)*   bag

*scythe *(n.)*   tool with a long handle and curved blade, used for cutting grass

*silver fox *(n.)*   a phase of the common red fox, which at a certain time of year has black fur tipped with white

*swipe *(n.)*   strong, sweeping blow

trickle *(v.)*   to flow slowly in a thin stream; to fall in drops

wheel *(v.)*   to push something on wheels

wheelbarrow *(n.)*   type of cart having a single wheel and handles for moving small loads

*white-washed *(adj.)*   covered with a white, paintlike liquid

Activities

1. Look closely at the text. What is life on the farm like for each of the characters? Make notes from the text to prove your point. Discuss your ideas with your class.

2. Look closely at the story. From whose point of view is the story being told? Make notes from the text to support your opinion.

3. How is the girl treated by each of her parents? What are their expectations of the boy Laird? How are these different from their expectations of the girl? Refer to specific passages in the story to support your opinion.

4. What are the girl's feelings toward her mother and her father? How does she feel about her brother Laird?

5. Write an essay describing the traditional roles for men and women in "Boys and Girls." Agree or disagree with this division of responsibilities by gender.

6. Using your notes, write an essay on the difficulties of farm life.

For Further Reading

Blodgett, E. D. *Alice Munro.* Boston: Twayne, 1988.

MacKendrick, Louis K., ed. *Probable Fictions: Alice Munro's Narrative Acts.* Downsview, ON: ECW, 1983.

Redekop, Magdalene. *Mothers and Other Clowns: The Stories of Alice Munro.* New York: Routledge, 1992.

Stouck, David. *Major Canadian Authors.* 2nd ed. Lincoln: U of Nebraska P, 1988.

23

From *Fire on the Mountain*

Anita Desai (b. 1937)
Fiction: Novel

Background

India is both a nation and a subcontinent. It is a multicultural area of at least 20 major language groups and three principal religious groups, Hindu, Muslim, and Buddhist. Since the early nineteenth century, this diverse area had been held together as a political unit by the British Empire. After a long period of struggle under the nonviolent leadership of Mohandas Gandhi, India gained independence from the British in 1947.

It was during the period of struggle against British rule that Anita Desai was born in 1937. She is representative of her multicultural nation in that her father was a Bengali and her mother a German. Fluent in both her parents' languages, Desai writes in English. In this way she gains a broad audience, since even in postcolonial India English is still the most commonly spoken language.

One of her country's leading contemporary women novelists, Desai added a new dimension to Anglo-Indian fiction by writing about the inner lives of her characters. That is, she focuses on the psychology of her characters, especially females, and reveals their private thoughts through unspoken monologues. In her work Desai also raises questions about the role of women in contemporary Indian society.

In addition, her novels and short stories frequently deal with aspects of the multicultural heritage of India. She is also concerned with the conflict between traditional Indian life, which is guided by Hindu and

Buddhist principles, and postindependence modern life. While the Indian leader Mohandas Gandhi encouraged a return to native Indian values, the impact of foreign occupation, especially under the British, has been enormous.

Desai's personal experiences mirror the multicultural situation of modern India. The autobiographical references and feminist perspective of her work echo an individual and national struggle for independence and identity.

In addition to *Fire on the Mountain* (1975), Anita Desai has written other successful novels such as *Clear Light of Day* (1980), *In Custody* (1980), and *Baumgartner's Bombay* (1988). In 1978 she received the National Academy of Letters Award. She presently lives and teaches in the United States.

Fire on the Mountain is the story of Nanda Kaul, an Indian great-grandmother who lives alone high in a Himalayan hill station. With only a servant to attend her, she fulfills her *dharma*, or destiny, with her solitary existence. Nanda Kaul is unable to understand the values of the younger generation and is quite disturbed when she learns that her great-grand-daughter Raka will be coming to stay with her. The novel describes their attempt to live together and their alienation from each other.

Pre-Reading Activities

1. With your study group, discuss what you think is the traditional role of women in the family. How do you see this traditional role changing?
2. With your study group, discuss the role of the elderly in traditional society. How is this role changing?

Key Terms

British Raj   Himalayan Mountains
Buddhism   Hindu/Hinduism
feminism/feminist   Indian independence (1947)
Gandhi, Mohandas (1869–1948)   Punjab

From *Fire on the Mountain*
Anita Desai

[Nanda Kaul] felt an enormous reluctance to open this letter.   1
She looked at it with **distaste** and **foreboding** for a long time before

Figure 24 • Indian woman in a garden
(Courtesy of Rita Narang)

she finally tore it open and drew out the bundle of dark blue pages across which [her daughter] Asha's large writing **pranced**. This writing had none of the writer's loveliness—it **sprawled** and spread and **shrieked** out loud an aggressive **assurance** and **aplomb**.

In this writing she conveyed a series of disasters and tragedies to her mother who read it through with her lips pressed so tightly together that it made deep lines **furrow** the skin from the corners of her nostrils to the corners of her mouth, dark **runnels** of disapproval. 2

"Darling Mama" (wrote Asha, and Nanda Kaul could scarcely believe that there had been a time when she was actually addressed as such and heard it quite naturally and calmly), "just a note this time as I'm in a mad rush. Now that I've persuaded Tara into going to Geneva [Switzerland] and Rakesh into taking her . . . well, I have to get Tara ready. This year's she's done *nothing*, Mama, just let herself go to **rack and ruin**, as well as her house—and poor little Raka, as you well know. . . . 3

"Poor little Raka looks like a ghost and hasn't quite got over her **typhoid** yet. She is very weak and the heat and humidity of 4

Bombay will do her no good. Everyone who sees her says she should go to the hills to recuperate. So Tara and I have decided it will be best to send her to you for the summer. Later, when Tara is settled in Geneva and has set up house, she will send for Raka.

"At the moment it is not possible for the child to travel or live   5
in an hotel. . . . We can't think of a better way for her to recuperate than spend a quiet summer with you in [Carignano]. And I know how happy it will make you to have your great-grandchild for company in that lonely house. . . ."

. . . Nanda Kaul narrowed her eyes as she went over the de-   6
tails of her great-grandchild's journey. Then she folded the blue sheets firmly, as if **suppressing** the hurry and rush of her daughter's excited plans, and slipped them back into the envelope. Placing it on her lap again, she looked out into the apricot trees, down the path to the gate, the cloudy **hydrangeas**, the pines scattering and hissing in the breeze. . . .

One long finger moved like a searching insect over the letter   7
on her lap, moved **involuntarily** as she struggled to suppress her anger, her disappointment and her total **loathing** of her daughter's meddling, **busybody** ways, her granddaughter [Tara's] **abject** helplessness, and her great-granddaughter's **impending** arrival here at Carignano.

She tried to divert her mind from these thoughts and concen-   8
trate on this well known and **perpetually** soothing scene. She tried to look on it as she had before the letter arrived, with pleasure and satisfaction. But she was too distracted now.

All she wanted was to be alone, to have Carignano to herself,   9
in this period of her life when stillness and calm were all that she wished to entertain.

Getting up at last, she went slowly round to the back of the   10
house and leant on the wooden railing on which the yellow rose creeper had blossomed so youthfully last month but was now reduced to an exhausted mass of grey creaks and groans again. She gazed down the **gorge** with its **gashes** of red earth, its rocks and **gullies** and sharply spiked **agaves**, to the Punjab plains—a silver haze in the summer heat—stretching out to a dim yellow horizon, and said Is it wrong? Have I not done enough and had enough? I want no more. I want nothing. Can I not be left with nothing? But there was no answer and of course she expected none.

Looking down, over all those years she had survived and   11
borne, she saw them, not bare and shining as the plains below, but like the gorge, **cluttered**, choked and blackened with the heads of

children and grandchildren, servants and guests, all restlessly surging, clamoring about her. . . .

Looking down at her knuckles, two rows of yellow bones on the railing, she thought of her sons and daughters, of her **confinements**, some in great discomfort at home and others at the small **filthy** missionary-run hospital . . . and the different nurses and doctors who had wanted to help her but never could, and the **slovenly**, neurotic **ayahs** she had had to have because there was such a deal of washing and ironing to do and Mr. Kaul had wanted her always in silk, at the head of the long **rosewood** table in the dining-room, entertaining his guests.

Mentally she **stalked** through the rooms of that house—his house, never hers—very carefully closing the wire-screen doors behind her to keep out the flies, looking sharply to see if the dark furniture, all rosewood, had been properly polished and the doors of the gigantic cupboards properly shut. . . .

Now, to **bow** again, to let that **noose** slip once more round her neck that she had thought was freed fully, finally. Now to have those **wails** and **bawls** shatter and rip her still house to pieces, to clutter the bare rooms. . . .

It seemed hard, it seemed unfair, when all she wanted was the sound of the **cicadas** and the pines, the sight of this gorge plunging, blood-red, down to the silver plain.

An eagle swept over it, far below her, a thousand feet below, its wings outspread, gliding on currents of air without once moving its great muscular wings which remained in **repose**, in control. She had wished, it occurred to her, to imitate that eagle—gliding with eyes closed.

Then a **cuckoo** called, quite close, here in her garden, very softly, very musically, but definitely calling—she recognized its domestic tone.

She gave that ironic **bow** again, very, very slightly, and went to the kitchen to see what Ram Lal had for lunch and tell him about the great-grandchild's visit.

Vocabulary

abject *(adj.)*   miserable; wretched
*agave *(n.)*   plant in the amaryllis family having tall flower stalks
*aplomb *(n.)*   complete, confident self-possession; poise

*Denotes low-frequency word.

assurance *(n.)*   confidence; certainty
***ayah** *(n.)*   nurse or maid native to India
***bawl** *(n.)*   loud cry that goes on for a long time
bow *(n.)*   bending in submission
bow *(v.)*   to yield; to submit
***busybody** *(adj.)*   concerned with other people's affairs
***cicada** *(n.)*   large, flylike insect, the male of which makes a loud, shrill
    sound
cluttered *(adj.)*   filled or covered with scattered things
***confinement** *(n.)*   state of being kept in bed or indoors because of
    illness or childbirth
***cuckoo** *(n.)*   bird whose call sounds somewhat like its name
distaste *(n.)*   dislike; aversion
filthy *(adj.)*   disgustingly dirty
***foreboding** *(n.)*   prediction, especially of something bad or harmful
***furrow** *(v.)*   to groove
***gash** *(n.)*   deep, narrow depression in the earth
***gorge** *(n.)*   narrow, steep-walled passage through land; canyon
***gully** *(n.)*   trench worn in the earth by running water after rains
***hydrangea** *(n.)*   plant with large, showy groups of white, pink, or blue
    flowers
impending *(adj.)*   about to occur
involuntarily *(adv.)*   not consciously controlled; automatically
loathing *(n.)*   great dislike
noose *(n.)*   loop formed in a rope that tightens as the rope is pulled; used
    to hang people
perpetually *(adv.)*   continuing forever
prance *(v.)*   to move in a spirited way
***rack and ruin** *(n.)*   poor state or condition
repose *(n.)*   state of rest
***rosewood** *(n.)*   valuable dark red or purplish wood used to make
    furniture
***runnel** *(n.)*   small stream
shriek *(v.)*   to cry out in a sharp, shrill sound; to suggest such a sound
slovenly *(adj.)*   untidy, especially in personal appearance
***sprawl** *(v.)*   to take up more space than is necessary
stalk *(v.)*   to walk stiffly or haughtily
suppress *(v.)*   to check; to keep back
***typhoid** *(n.)*   serious disease contracted from polluted water and marked
    by high fever
wail *(n.)*   cry expressing dissatisfaction or complaint that goes on for a
    long time

*Denotes low-frequency word.

Activities

1. Look closely at the text. With your group or alone, make notes on how Nanda Kaul feels about her great-grandchild's visit. How does the author reveal Nanda Kaul's feelings to the reader? Support your answer with specific lines from the text. Discuss your ideas with the class.

2. How does the author use nature in this passage? In what way is it Romantic?

3. Based on your notes and discussion, write an essay on the conflict Nanda Kaul feels over her role as a woman.

4. Based on your notes and discussion, write an essay on the role of the elderly in modern society. Support your points with specific details.

For Further Reading

Bande, Usha. *The Novels of Anita Desai.* New Delhi: Prestige, 1988.

Dhawan, R. K., ed. *The Fiction of Anita Desai.* New Delhi: Bahri, 1989.

Embree, Ainslie T. *India's Search for National Identity.* New Delhi: Chanakya, 1980.

Watson, Francis. *A Concise History of India.* London: Thames, 1979.

Zimmer, Heinrich. *Myths and Symbols in Indian Art and Civilization.* Ed. Joseph Campbell. 2nd ed. Princeton: Princeton UP, 1974.

24

From *The Thief and the Dogs*

Naguib Mahfouz (b. 1911)
Fiction: Novel

Background

      The son of middle-class Muslim parents, Naguib Mahfouz lived for the first six years of his life in the crowded, conservative Islamic old quarter of Cairo, Egypt. His family then moved to the modern, Europeanized suburb of Abbasiyah, where he witnessed firsthand the Egyptian struggle for independence from the British. He later attended the University of Cairo, where he studied philosophy and read the works of Western intellectuals such as Darwin, Marx, Nietzsche, and Freud. All of these contrasting experiences have influenced Mahfouz's novels.

      Mahfouz combined a long career as an Egyptian civil servant with serious writing, earning a reputation as one of the most outstanding and gifted novelists in the Arabic-speaking world today. Mahfouz has been a highly prolific author, writing an average of one book per year, dozens of movie scripts, and a weekly political column in an Egyptian-language newspaper.

      Although Arabic literature has a long history, its major forms have been the short story and poetry, both closely associated with a rich oral tradition. Mahfouz was the first successful creator of the modern Arabic novel. His early literary influences were drawn from important European sources such as the Romanticism of Victor Hugo, the Realism of Charles Dickens, and the internal monologue of James Joyce and Virginia Woolf. In 1988 he received the Nobel Prize in literature and was cited as forming "an Arabic narrative art that applies to all mankind."

The earliest novels written by Mahfouz were historical works about the rich ancient Egyptian past. But for some time after the 1952 Egyptian revolution led by Colonel Gamal Abdel Nasser, Naguib Mahfouz did not write fiction. He first received broad public recognition in the Arab world after the publication of his 1,200-page *Cairo Trilogy* (1956–1957). Mahfouz's 1959 Existentialist novel, *Children of Gebelawi*, was an allegorical story of religious crisis that reflected the pessimism of Egypt's intellectuals at that time. The work was poorly received by traditional Islamic readers. His next novel, *The Thief and the Dogs*, was published in 1961 and was well received. Using the stream-of-consciousness technique and interior monologue in this novel, Mahfouz reveals the mind of an Egyptian man seeking to destroy the individuals and the society he believes have condemned him to damnation. Although the protagonist, Said, tries to save himself by returning to the mystic influence of a sheikh and his childhood religion, his complete alienation and desire for revenge make it impossible for him to renew his faith.

Pre-Reading Activities

1. Why do you think people sometimes return to the places and memories of their childhood? Discuss your ideas with your group.
2. What is moral behavior? How do you believe children learn about moral behavior? Discuss your ideas with your group.

Key Terms

allusion	Koran
Arab/Arabic	Muslim
Cairo Trilogy	mystic
Egyptian revolution (1952)	Said [sah-eed] Mahran
historical novel	sheikh
Islam	stream-of-consciousness technique

From *The Thief and the Dogs*
Naguib Mahfouz

At the **threshold** of the open door [Said] paused, trying to   1
remember when he'd crossed it last. The simplicity of the house, which could hardly be different from those of Adam's day, was **striking**. At the left corner of the big, open courtyard stood a tall palm

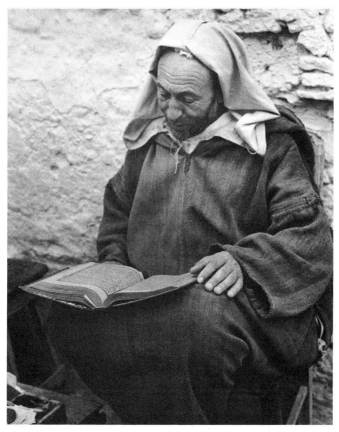

Figure 25 • Moslem holy man reading the Koran *(© 1984 Eugene Gordon/Photo Researchers)*

tree with a crooked top; to the right an entrance corridor led by an open door—in this strange house no door was ever closed—to a single room.

His heart beat fast, carrying him back to a distant, gentle time   2 of childhood, dreams, a loving father, and his own innocent **yearning**. He recalled the men filling the courtyard, **swaying** with their **chanting**, God's praise echoing from the depths of their hearts. "Look and listen, learn and open your heart," his father used to say.

Besides a joy like the joy of Paradise that was aroused in him   3 by faith and dreams, there had also been the joy of singing and green tea. . . .

From inside the room he could hear a man concluding his   4 prayers. Said smiled, slipped in carrying his books, and saw the Sheikh sitting cross-legged on the prayer carpet, absorbed in quiet

recitation. The old room had hardly changed. The **rush mats** had been replaced by new ones, thanks to his **disciples**, but the Sheikh's sleeping mattress still lay close to the western wall, pierced by the window through which the rays of the declining sun were pouring down at Said's feet. The other walls of the room were half covered with rows of books on shelves. The odor of incense **lingered** as if it were the same he remembered, never **dissipated**, from years ago. Putting down his load of books, he approached the Sheikh.

"Peace be upon you, my lord and master."   5

Having completed his recitation, the Sheikh raised his head,   6
disclosing a face that was **emaciated** but radiant with overflowing vitality, framed by a white beard like a **halo**, and surmounted by a white **skullcap** that **nestled** in thick **locks** of hair showing silvery at his temples.

The Sheikh **scrutinized** him with eyes that had been viewing   7
this world for eighty years and indeed had **glimpsed** the next, eyes that had not lost their appeal, acuteness, or charm. Said found himself bending over his hand to kiss it, suppressing tears of nostalgia for his father, his boyish hopes, the innocent purity of the distant past.

"Peace and God's compassion be upon you," said the Sheikh   8
in a voice like Time.

What had his father's voice been like? He could see his father's   9
face and his lips moving, and tried to make his eyes do the service of ears, but the voice had gone. . . .

Did the Sheikh remember him? "Forgive my coming to your   10
house like this. But there's nowhere else in the world for me to go."
. . . [N]ot knowing what to say, [Said] sighed, then quietly remarked, "I got out of jail today."

"Jail?" said the Sheikh, his eyes closed.   11

"Yes. You haven't seen me for more than ten years, and dur-   12
ing that time strange things have happened to me. . . . In any case, I didn't want to meet you under **false pretenses**, so I'm telling you I got out of jail, only today."

The Sheikh slowly shook his head, then, opening his eyes, said,   13
"You have not come from jail." The voice was sorrowful.

Said smiled. This was the language of old times again, where   14
words had a double meaning. . . .

Fairly certain that he was remembered, Said asked for **reas-**   15
surance: "And do you remember my father, Mr. Mahran, God have mercy upon his soul?"

"May God have mercy upon all of us."   16

"What wonderful days those were!"   17

"Say that, if you can, about the present."   18

"But . . ."   19

"God have mercy upon all of us."   20

"I was saying, I just got out of jail today."   21

he was **impaled** on the stake he smiled and said, 'It was God's will that I should meet Him thus.' "

    . . . "Master, I have come to you now when my own daughter   23
has **rejected** me."

    The Sheikh sighed. "God reveals His secrets to His tiniest crea- 24
tures!"

    "I thought that if God had granted you long life, I would find 25
your door open."

    "And the door of Heaven? How have you found that?"   26

    "But there is nowhere on earth for me to go. And my own   27
daughter has rejected me."

    "How like you she is!"   28

    "In what way, Master?"   29

    "You seek a roof, not an answer."   30

    . . . "I am in need of a kind word," Said pleaded.   31

    "Do not tell lies." The Sheikh spoke gently, then bowed his   32
head, his beard **fanning out** over his chest, and seemed lost in thought. . . . Suddenly the Sheikh said, "Take a copy of the **Koran** and read."

    A little confused, Said explained apologetically, "I just got out 33
of jail today, and I have not performed the prayer **ablutions**."

    "Wash yourself now and read."   34

    "My own daughter has rejected me. She was scared of me, as   35
if I was the devil. And before that her mother was unfaithful to me."

    "Wash and read," replied the Sheikh gently.   36

    "She committed adultery with one of my men, a **layabout**, a 37
mere pupil of mine, utterly **servile**. She applied for divorce on grounds of my imprisonment and went and married him."

    "Wash and read."   38

    "And he took everything I owned, the money and the jewelry.   39
He's a big man now, and all the local crooks have become followers and **cronies** of his."

    "Wash and read."   40

    "It wasn't thanks to any sweat by the police that I was ar-   41
rested." Said went on, the veins in his forehead **pulsing** with anger. "No, it wasn't. I was sure of my safety, as usual. It was that dog who

betrayed me, in **collusion** with her. Then disaster followed disaster until finally my daughter rejected me."

"Wash and read the verses: 'Say to them: if you love God, then   42
follow me and God will love you' and 'I have chosen thee for Myself.' Also repeat the words: 'Love is acceptance, which means obeying His commands and refraining from what He has prohibited and contentment with what He **decrees** and **ordains.**' "

. . . *[T]he sun is not yet set. The last golden thread is **receding** from*   43
*the window. A long night is waiting for me, the first night of freedom. I am alone with my freedom, or rather I'm in the company of the Sheikh, who is lost in heaven, repeating words that cannot be understood by someone approaching hell. What other **refuge** have I?*

Vocabulary

*****ablution** *(n.)*   washing of one's body or part of it, as in a religious
    ceremony
chanting *(n.)*   reciting in a repetitive way
collusion *(n.)*   secret agreement or cooperation
*****crony** *(n.)*   close friend
decree *(v.)*   to command
disciple *(n.)*   one who accepts and assists in spreading the doctrines of
    another
dissipate *(v.)*   to dissolve; to spread out to the point of vanishing
emaciated *(adj.)*   very thin
*****false pretense** *(n.)*   deliberate misrepresentation of fact
*****fanning out** *(adj.)*   spreading out like a fan
glimpse *(v.)*   to get a brief look at
halo *(n.)*   circle of light, especially around the head, showing holiness
impale *(v.)*   to kill or torture by fixing on a sharp, pointed stick
Koran *(n.)*   book of sacred writings accepted by Muslims as revelations to
    Mohammed by Allah through the angel Gabriel
*****layabout** *(n.)*   lazy person
linger *(v.)*   to remain although in a weakened form
lock *(n.)*   tuft; clump
mere *(adj.)*   being nothing more than
nestle *(v.)*   to sit comfortably or snugly
ordain *(v.)*   to order
pulsing *(adj.)*   beating; throbbing
reassurance *(n.)*   new assurance
recede *(v.)*   to move back or away

*Denotes low-frequency word.

recitation *(n.)*   the act of reading or repeating aloud
refuge *(n.)*   shelter or protection from distress or danger
reject *(v.)*   to refuse to accept
*rush mat *(n.)*   rug made of grasses
scrutinize *(v.)*   to examine closely
servile *(adj.)*   slavelike; exhibiting submissive behavior
*skullcap *(n.)*   close-fitting cap without a brim
striking *(adj.)*   attracting attention because of remarkable qualities
swaying *(adj.)*   moving from side to side
*threshold *(n.)*   doorsill
yearning *(n.)*   deep or anxious longing or desire

Activities

1. In your journal, make notes about Said's feelings as he returns to the Sheikh's house. How are the feelings he had as a child different from those he feels now?

2. Said is a criminal pursued by the police. Why do you believe he has returned to the Sheikh's house? What does he want?

3. What is the "double meaning" of the Sheikh's words? Why are the Sheikh and Said not communicating?

4. Write an essay explaining or elaborating on the importance of religious or moral education. Give specific examples to support your argument.

5. Write an essay on the reasons for the lack of communication between the Sheikh and Said in Mahfouz's story.

For Further Reading

Beard, Michael, and Adnan Haydar, eds. *Naguib Mahfouz: From Regional Fame to Global Recognition.* Syracuse: Syracuse UP, 1992.

Gordon, Hayim. *Naguib Mahfouz's Egypt: Existential Themes in His Writings.* New York: Greenwood, 1990.

Kessler, Brad. "Laureate in the Land of the Pharaohs." *New York Times Magazine* 3 June 1990: 38+.

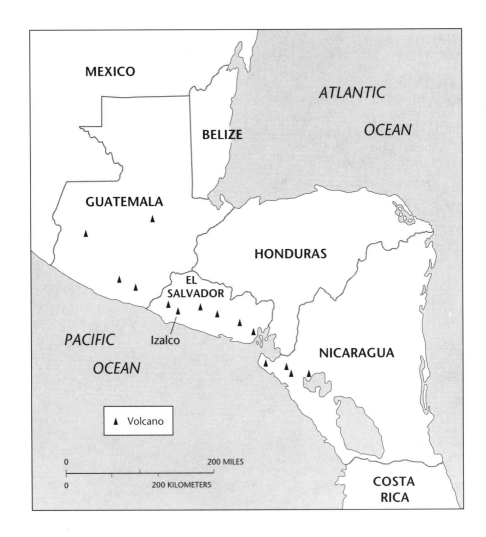

MEXICO

ATLANTIC

OCEAN

BELIZE

GUATEMALA ▲

▲

HONDURAS

▲
▲ EL
SALVADOR
▲
▲ ▲ ▲
▲
PACIFIC Izalco
▲
OCEAN NICARAGUA
▲
▲ ▲

▲ Volcano

0   200 MILES

0   200 KILOMETERS

COSTA
RICA

Figure 26 • Map of Central America with volcanoes

25

From *Flowers from the Volcano*

Claribel Alegría (b. 1924)
Oral Tradition and Poetry: Free Verse

Background

Born in Nicaragua, Central America, Claribel Alegría experienced political exile at the age of nine when her father was forced to leave their country and moved his family to El Salvador. At age 19 she arrived in the United States to study philosophy at George Washington University. After graduating, she married Darwin Flakoll.

Violence plays an important role in much of Alegría's work. She identifies the violence of the volcanic Meso-American landscape with a tradition of human violence. She acknowledges the violent behavior of pre-Columbian indigenous cultures such as the Aztec as well as the violence and destruction associated with the arrival of Christopher Columbus in the New World. Although sixteenth-century Spanish priests such as Fray Diego de Landa tried to protect the native culture, the European presence has had a major impact. As a result, the native Indian population finds itself marginalized in its own land. The present violence continues not only in the giant volcano Izalco, threatening to explode at any moment, but in the torture and mass murder of Indian peasants by terrorists.

In reaction to the horrors of Central American government terrorism against poor peasants seeking a better life, Claribel Alegría has looked to socialist and Marxist philosophy. In her life and in her writing, she has consistently spoken out about the struggle for liberation of the oppressed in Central America.

Alegría has published 14 books of poetry, as well as novellas and children's stories. Much of her work has been translated from Spanish into English by her husband. Claribel Alegría and her husband presently live in Managua, Nicaragua, and Mallorca, Spain.

Pre-Reading Activities

1. With your class, discuss the role of the poet in politics. Should the poet write only about "beauty," or about real-life issues as well?
2. Locate Central America on a map. What is the area like? How could the geography influence life there?

Key Terms

Aztecs and Incas	marginal/marginalized
Central America	Marxism/Marxist
chacmol	Maya/Mayan
Columbus, Christopher (1451–1506)	Meso-America
de Landa, Fray Diego (1524–1579)	mestizo
human sacrifice	pre-Columbian
indigenous culture	Tlaloc (also called Chac)

"Flowers from the Volcano"

Claribel Alegría

To Roberto and Ana Maria

Fourteen volcanos rise
in my remembered country
in my mythical country.
Fourteen volcanos of **foliage** and stone
where strange clouds hold back   5
the **screech** of a homeless bird.
Who said that my country was green?
It is more red, more gray, more violent:
Izalco roars,
taking more lives.   10
Eternal **Chacmol** collects blood,
the gray **orphans**
the volcano spitting bright lava

Figure 27   •   Mayan chacmol

and the dead ***guerrillero***
and the thousand **betrayed** faces,   15
the children who are watching
so they can tell of it.
Not one kingdom was left us.
One by one they fell
through all the Americas.   20
Steel rang in palaces,
in the streets,
in the forests
and the **centaurs sacked** the temple.
Gold disappeared and continues   25
to disappear on ***yanqui*** ships,
the golden coffee mixed with blood.
The priest flees screaming
in the middle of the night
he calls his followers   30
and they open the *guerrillero's* chest

so as to offer the **Chac**
his smoking heart.
No one believes in Izalco
that **Tlaloc** is dead   35
despite television,
refrigerators,
Toyotas.
The cycle is closing,
strange the volcano's silence   40
since it last drew breath.
Central America trembled,
Managua collapsed.
In Guatemala the earth sank
Hurricane Fifi flattened Honduras.   45
They say the *yanquis* turned it away,
that it was moving toward Florida
and they forced it back.
The golden coffee is unloaded
in New York where   50
they roast it, grind it
can it and give it a price.
Siete de Junio
noche fatal
bailando el tango   55
la capital.
[Seventh of June
fatal night
dancing the tango
in the capital.]
From the shadowed terraces
San Salvador's volcano rises.
Two-story **mansions**
protected by walls   60
four meters high
march up its **flanks**
each with **railings** and gardens,
roses from England
and dwarf *araucarias*,   65
Uruguayan pines.
Farther up, in the **crater**
within the crater's walls
live peasant families

who cultivate flowers   70
their children can sell.
The cycle is closing,
Cuscatlecan flowers
thrive in volcanic ash,
they grow strong, tall, brilliant.   75
The volcano's children
flow down like lava
with their bouquets of flowers,
like roots they **meander**
like rivers the cycle is closing.   80
The owners of two-story houses
protected from thieves by walls
peer from their balconies
and they see the red waves descending
and they drown their fears in whiskey.   85
They are only children in rags
with flowers from the volcano,
with *Jacintos* and *Pascuas* and *Mulatas*
but the wave is **swelling**,
today's Chacmol still wants blood,   90
the cycle is closing,
Tlaloc is not dead.

Vocabulary

*araucania (n.)   flower native to Central America
betrayed (adj.)   deceived
*centaur (n.)   mythical creature said to be half man and half horse
   (referring here to the Spanish conquerors mounted on horseback)
*Chac (prop. n.)   Mayan raingod, portrayed with a long nose resembling a
   rainspout
*Chacmol (n.)   Mayan stone altar in the form of a reclining man holding
   a bowl to receive the hearts of human sacrifices
*crater (n.)   bowl-shaped area around the opening of a volcano
*Cuscatlecan (adj.) (Mayan)   belonging to Cuscatlan, "Land of the
   Jewel," capital and territory of the Pipil native tribe, a group culturally
   like the Aztecs
flank (n.)   side
foliage (n.)   leaves

---

*Denotes low-frequency word.

*guerrillero *(n.) (Spanish)*   fighter

*Izalco *(prop. n.) (Mayan)*   "Lighthouse of the Pacific"; a 6,183-foot-high volcano in El Salvador that has been active intermittently since the eighteenth century

*Jacintos, Pascuas, and **Mulatas** *(prop. n.) (Spanish)*   here, the names of flowers as well as children

mansion *(n.)*   large, impressive house

meander *(v.)*   to wander without direction

orphan *(n.)*   child whose parents have died

peer *(v.)*   to look curiously at something

*railing *(n.)*   fence consisting of posts with a bar across the top

sack *(v.)*   to strip of valuables; to loot

screech *(n.)*   high, shrill piercing cry (as a symbol, the Mayan screeching bird is associated with the end of the universe)

*Siete de Junio (Seventh of June)   Salvadoran song popular during the 1917 volcanic eruption of Izalco

swell *(v.)*   to expand; to get bigger

thrive *(v.)*   to grow very well

*Tlaloc *(prop. n.)*   Mayan god of rain and sacrifice whose written symbol, or glyph, is a sign of war and bloodletting

*yanqui *(n.) (Spanish)*   North American person

Activities

1. With your small group or class, read the poem "Flowers from the Volcano" aloud. What evidence of oral tradition do you see in the poem?

2. Make notes in your journal about the way Alegría uses the image of flowers in the poem. What do they symbolize? How do the rich respond to them? What do you think the poem's title means? Discuss your ideas with your class.

3. Read the poem again, making notes in your journal about the way Alegría uses myth to compare the past and the present. What does she imply will happen in the future? Discuss your ideas with your group.

4. What is the purpose of Alegría's poem "Flowers from the Volcano"? What feelings does she want her audience to experience? What does she expect her audience to do? Support your point of view with specific lines from the poem.

5. Write an essay based on your notes and discussion on Claribel Alegría's use of myth in "Flowers from the Volcano."

6. Write an essay arguing for or against poetry with a political message.

---

*Denotes low-frequency word.

For Further Reading

Flakoll, Darwin, and Claribel Alegría, eds. *New Voices of Hispanic America: An Anthology*. Boston: Beacon, 1962.

McClintock, Michael. *The American Connection: State Terror and Popular Resistance in El Salvador*. London: Zed, 1985.

Rojas, Mario A. "Some Central American Writers of Liberation," In *Culture, Human Rights and Peace in Central America*. Ed. George F. McLean et al. Lanham: UP of America, 1989.

Santos, Rosario, ed. *And We Sold the Rain: Contemporary Fiction from Central America*. New York: Four Walls Eight Windows, 1988.

Schele, Linda, and David Freidel. *A Forest of Kings: The Untold Story of the Ancient Maya*. New York: Morrow, 1990.

Additional Reading

Sacred Hymn of Sacrifice to Tlaloc[†]

Anonymous (fifteenth century)
Oral Tradition and Poetry: Sacred Text

Background

Two sixteenth-century Spanish priests observed and recorded in great detail the cultures of the indigenous Aztecs and Mayans they encountered in Mesoamerica. One, Fray Bernardino de Sahagún, arrived in Mexico in 1529 and wrote a multivolume work entitled *General History of the Things of New Spain*, which included native hymns and prayers. Another priest, Fray Diego de Durán, detailed the oral tradition as well as the written codices, or painted books, that preserved Aztec and Mayan traditions. Fray Diego describes the dramatic religious ceremony of the sacrifice of a seven-year-old girl to Tlaloc to ensure the fertility of the maize crop:

> The feast of [Tlaloc] took place on the twenty-ninth of April and was so solemn and important that every king and lord, the old and the young, all came with their offerings from every part of the land. . . . It was devoted to petitioning a good year for the maize which was already sprouting. . . . The priests took out the child who . . . was all dressed in blue, which represented the great lake and all the fountains and small rivers, with a band of reddish leather around her head and fastened to it a tuft of blue

feather. . . . Facing the idol . . . they brought a drum and all
sat down without dancing, with the girl in front, and they sang
many and varied songs. (Quoted in Leon-Portilla, 99–100)

Sacred Hymn of Sacrifice to Tlaloc
Anonymous

CHORUS: In Mexico we beg a loan from the god.   1
   There are the banners of paper
   and at the four corners
   men are standing.

PRIEST OF TLALOC: Now, Tlaloc, it is time for you to weep!   5
   Alas, I [the child] was created
   and for my god
   festal bundles of blood-stained ears of corn
   I carry now
   to the divine hearth.   10
   You are my chief, Prince and Magician,
   and though in truth
   it is you who produces our sustenance,
   although you are the first,
   we only cause you shame.   15

TLALOC (A MASKED PRIEST): If anyone
   has caused me shame,
   it is because he did not know me well;
   [he did not know my power];
   you are my fathers, my priests,   20
   Serpents and Tigers.

CHORUS [speaking in the name of the child victim]:
   I will go away forever,
   it is time for crying.
   Send me to the Place of Mystery,   25
   under your command.
   I have already told
   the Prince of the Sad Omen,
   I will go away forever,
   it is time for crying.   30
   In four years
   comes the arising among us,
   many people

without knowing it;
in the place of the fleshless,   35
the house of quetzal feathers,
is the transformation.
It is the act of the Propagator of Men.

PRIEST OF TLALOC: Go to all parts
spread out . . .   40
in the region of mist.
With [clouds] of mist
our word is carried to the house of Tlaloc.

Fray Diego continues his account of the sacrificial ritual:

> After this hymn, dances and other songs were offered to the rain
> god. The priests then took the child victim in a boat to the center
> of the lake where they sacrificed her, letting her blood and a num-
> ber of jewels fall into the water. The ritual drama with songs,
> dances and costumes, asking Tlaloc for life-giving rain, had been
> acted out. (Leon-Portilla, 100–03)

Activities

1. Choose one or two symbols in this religious ritual and explain their
   meaning and significance in an essay.
2. Reread the poem "Flowers from the Volcano." What does the poet
   mean when she states that "Tlaloc is not dead"?
3. Compare the child in the religious ritual to the children in the poem
   "Flowers from the Volcano."

For Further Reading

Leon-Portilla, Miguel. *Pre-Columbian Literatures of Mexico.* Trans. Grace
     Lobanov and Miguel Leon-Portilla. Norman: U of Oklahoma P, 1986.
Morley, Sylvanus G., and George W. Brainerd. *The Ancient Maya.* Rev.
     Robert J. Sharer. 4th ed. Stanford: Stanford UP, 1983.

26

From *Praisesong for the Widow*

Paule Marshall (b. 1929)
Fiction: Novel

Background

The earliest West Indian literary sources originate in Africa and are part of oral tradition. However, much of the eighteenth- and nineteenth-century West Indian literature is based on European models. For example, among the early written works are slave narratives similar to the European picaresque novels. Such narratives recount the life of an African taken from home by force, sold into slavery, and shipped to the Caribbean or to North America.

The contemporary period, which includes the work of Paule Marshall, has included a focus on the quest for identity through a journey to the white Western world (England or the United States) and then to Africa before a return home, approximating the experience of the Middle Passage. Like the ancient epic hero, the protagonist gains wisdom and pride to be shared with others.

Although Paule Marshall was born and educated in Brooklyn, New York, her parents are from Barbados, a small island in the West Indies in the Caribbean. Marshall has lived in Barbados while working on her writing and, therefore, exhibits a strong West Indian influence in her work. In her rich descriptive passages, Marshall evokes the tropical landscape of the Caribbean. Furthermore, her dialogues reflect West Indian idioms and dialect, and she uses the rhythms of Afro-Caribbean music to evoke a closeness with mother earth.

Marshall's first novel, *Brown Girl, Brownstones* (1959), is the story of a Barbadian immigrant girl whose parents struggle to preserve their ethnic heritage in the assimilation process. Her 1983 novel, *Praisesong for the Widow*, describes the journey of an unhappy, assimilated African-American woman to discover her ethnic roots. An affluent, middle-aged widow, Avey Johnson takes a vacation cruise to the Caribbean. She unexpectedly relives the terrible Middle Passage her ancestors experienced when they were brought across the Atlantic Ocean to the New World as slaves to work on sugar plantations. An appreciation of her rich African heritage brings new meaning to Avey's life.

Throughout her work, Marshall contrasts the potential destructive power of Western technology with Afro-Caribbean harmony with the natural world. The reader is made aware of the tremendous human and ecological cost of materialism and "progress." Without seeming to preach, Marshall clearly indicates that the American dream of relentlessly pursuing materialism may result in the sacrifice of moral or ethical principles. She reminds us that the traditions of the past still have a place in the contemporary world.

Pre-Reading Activities

1. What do you think are some of the reasons people leave their country for a new one? Is the departure always voluntary? How would someone's reasons for being in a new land affect their feelings about their old and new countries?

2. In your study group, discuss what you feel might be some of the reasons people would want to know about their ethnic heritage.

3. What does it mean to be a tourist? What is the difference between visiting a place as a tourist and returning to a place associated with one's ancestors?

Key Terms

assimilation	feminist movement
Barbados/Barbadian/Bajan	Harlem Renaissance
Caribbean	materialism
civil rights movement	Middle Passage
ecological harmony	slave narrative
ethnic heritage	West Indies/West Indian

Figure 28   •   Cruise ship in port *(Fritz Menle/Photo Researchers)*

From *Praisesong for the Widow*
Paule Marshall

With a strength born of the decision that had just come to her   1
in the middle of the night, Avey Johnson forced the suitcase shut on
the clothes piled inside and slid the lock into place. Taking care not to
make a sound, she then eased the heavy bag off the couch onto the
floor and, straining under her breath, her tall figure bent almost in
two, **hauled** it over the thick carpeting to the door on the other side
of the cabin. . . .

From the moment she had awakened in a panic less than an   2
hour ago and come to the reckless decision, her mind had left to go
and stand down at the embarkation door near the waterline five
decks below. While she swiftly **criss-crossed** the room on her bare
feet, **spiriting** her belongings out of the closet and drawers, her
mind had leaped ahead to the time, later that morning, when the
ship would have arrived at the next **port of call**. . . . [A]long with
her fellow passengers going ashore for the day, she would step from

the **liner** onto the waiting **launch**. For the last time. And without so much as a backward glance.

Avey Johnson's two traveling companions, with whom she   3
shared the large deluxe cabin, were asleep in the bedroom on the other side of a divider with narrow shelflike openings on top and a long chest of drawers below, facing what was called the living area. Not to risk waking them, she had left off the lamps in the living area, where she always volunteered to sleep each cruise because it was more private. . . .

Slipping back over to the couch, her feet struck a chair. Quickly   4
she **stifled** her outcry, shook off the pain and kept going. When was the last time she had gone barefoot around the house? . . . Halsey Street? Had it been that long ago?

Back then the young woman whose headstrong ways and high   5
feelings Avey Johnson had long put behind her, whom she found an embarrassment to even think of now with her 1940s **upsweeps** and pompadours and **vampish** high-heeled shoes, used to kick off her shoes the moment she came in from work. . . . The 78 [records] on the turntable in the living room: Coleman Hawkins, Lester Young, The Count, The Duke. Music to usher Jay in the door. Freed of the high-heels her body always felt restored to its proper **axis**. . . . And the floor **reverberating** with "Cottontail" and "Lester Leaps In" would be like a rich nurturing ground from which she had sprung and to which she could always turn for sustenance. . . .

She was down to the last of the six suitcases.   6

"But why six, Mother? Why would anyone in their right mind   7
need to take this much stuff just to go away for a couple of weeks?"—Marion, Avey Johnson's youngest, the morning she had come to drive her mother to the pier before her first cruise three years ago. Entering the house, Marion had stopped short at sight of the half-dozen bags neatly lined up in the downstairs hall, had stood staring at them for the longest time, trying to contain her exasperation but failing. When she finally looked up it had been all she could do, from her expression, not to reach out and grab her mother by the shoulders and shake her the way she might have one of her pupils in the small community school she helped run in a church in Brooklyn. To shake sense into her. Around the face which **bore** [her father] Jay's clear imprint, her hair had stood **massed** like a raincloud about to **make good its threat**. And the noisy necklace of **cowrie shells** and **amber** she had brought back from Togo her last visit had sounded her angry despair with its rattle each time she breathed.

"Why go on some meaningless cruise with a bunch of white   8 folks anyway, I keep asking you? What's that supposed to be about? Couldn't you think of something better to do on your vacation? And since when have you started letting Thomasina Moore decide how you should spend it? You don't even like the woman. . . ."

. . . [W]hatever doubts [Marion] had managed to **sow** in Avey   9
Johnson's mind vanished the moment she saw the *Bianca Pride* that first time in her **berth** at West Fortieth Street and the river, with the flags and pennants flying from all her stations, her high bow **canted** toward the sun. All that dazzling white steel! Her **hull** appeared to sweep clear across to New Jersey. . . . Her group had stood awestruck and **reverent** before the [ship's] **console** with its array of keyboards, switches and closed circuit television screens. . . .

The marathon packing was done. On an armchair near the   10
window lay the clothes she had hastily set aside to wear. The suit-cases, all six of them along with the shoe **caddy** and hat box, stood assembled near the door, ready for the steward. Giving the **apprehensive** glance over her shoulder, she immediately headed toward them, not even allowing herself a moment to rest her back or wipe the perspiration from her face—or to consider, quietly and rationally, which was normally her way, what she was about to do.

Outside the glow of the deck lights was slowly being absorbed   11
by a pearl-gray light that was both filtering down from the clearing sky and curling up like mist from the sea. And the sea itself had become a wide, silvertoned sheet of **plate metal**, which was already, out near the horizon, reflecting the subtle mauve and rose and pale yellows of the day.

Amid the **burgeoning** color stood the liner—huge, sleek, im-   12
perial, a **glacial** presence in the warm waters of the Caribbean. The long night run completed, it had come to rest and drop anchor a short time ago in the same smooth and soundless manner with which it had moved over the sea.

From its decks could be made out the faint, almost **insubstan-**   13
tial form of an island across the silvery **moat** of the harbor. The next port of call.

Avey Johnson had finished in good time.   14

Vocabulary

amber *(n.)*   hard yellow or brown fossil material that can be polished and is used chiefly in making jewelry

apprehensive *(adj.)*   anticipating with anxiety, dread, or fear

axis *(n.)*   line of orientation

bear (bore, borne) *(v.)*   to carry
***berth** *(n.)*   place for a ship at a dock
***bianca** *(adj.) (Italian)*   white
***burgeoning** *(adj.)*   growing and expanding rapidly
***caddy** *(n.)*   container for holding objects when not in use
***canted** *(adj.)*   inclined; tilted
console *(n.)*   panel; cabinet
***cowrie shell** *(n.)*   glossy, often brightly colored shell found in warm
    seas, formerly used as a form of money in Africa
criss-cross *(v.)*   to move back and forth across
glacial *(adj.)*   like a glacier (a large mass of ice)
haul *(v.)*   to pull
***hull** *(n.)*   body of a ship
insubstantial *(adj.)*   lacking substance, firmness, or solidity
launch *(n.)*   boat that takes people to and from a ship
liner *(n.)*   passenger ship
make good its threat *(v. phrase)*   to carry out something negative that
    was impending
massed *(adj.)*   collected; formed
***moat** *(n.)*   channel of water, usually around a castle
***plate metal** *(n.)*   smooth, flat, thin piece of metal
port of call *(n.)*   harbor town where cruise ships stop
reverberating *(adj.)*   echoing
reverent *(adj.)*   worshipful
sow *(v.)*   to introduce; to implant
spiriting *(adj.)*   carrying out secretly
stifle *(v.)*   to hold back
***upsweep** *(n.)*   1940s hairstyle with the hair combed up and piled on top
    of the head
***vampish** *(adj.)*   seductive

Activities

1. Notice that the author moves between the recent past (as in the first
   three paragraphs) and the more distant past (paragraphs 5 and 7–9).
   As you read, try to figure out the relationship between events in the
   distant past and in the recent past.

2. What is Avey Johnson's daughter Marion like? What specific details
   does Marshall use to describe her? How do we know Marion is proud
   of her African heritage?

3. What do you think Marion's view is of her mother's taking a cruise to
   the Caribbean? What is Avey Johnson's view of her cruise? What values are important to her when she takes her first cruise?

*Denotes low-frequency word.

4. Marshall uses the cruise ship as a symbol of mainstream white American culture. In your journal, analyze the presentation of the inside and outside of the cruise ship. What are the specific details and images that Marshall provides? What do you think she is saying about American culture?

5. Contrast the image of the cruise ship with the ships that brought most Africans through the Middle Passage to America. Why is it ironic that Avey Johnson takes her vacations on a cruise ship?

6. In your journal, make notes about the details Marshall gives to describe Afro-Caribbean culture. How does Afro-Caribbean culture contrast in the story with white American values?

7. Inferring from the selection, write an essay on why you think Avey Johnson has decided to abandon the Caribbean cruise.

8. Write an essay arguing for or against the importance of learning about one's ethnic heritage.

For Further Reading

Cartey, Wilfred. *Whispers from the Caribbean: I Going Away, I Going Home.* Los Angeles: U of California P, 1991.

Lewis, Gordon K. *Main Currents in Caribbean Thought.* Baltimore: Johns Hopkins UP, 1983.

Glossary of
Literary Terms

action or **plot**   The events that happen in a narrative or play.

antagonist   A character who opposes the main character.

ballad   A narrative poem in quatrains (groups of four lnes), with the second and fourth lines rhyming.

character   A person appearing in a work of literature; also, the personality of an individual.

chorus   A group of actors in a Greek tragedy who represent the community; they comment on the action and advise the characters.

comedy   A play with a happy ending; something funny.

epic   A long narrative poem focusing on a central character; sometimes called a **heroic poem**.

epithet   A standard word or phrase describing a god or person, such as "godlike Odysseus."

framed story   A story within a story, usually told by one of the characters.

genre   A literary form, such as the novel or poem.

Gothic tale   A literary form popular at the end of the eighteenth and beginning of the nineteenth century. It is characterized by use of the supernatural, images of dark and mysterious castles, ghosts, and other terrifying phenomena.

lyric   A short poem of strong feeling or emotion, originally sung to the accompaniment of the lyre (a stringed musical instrument).

Magical Realism   A Latin American literary movement begun in the 1960s that stressed an imaginative reality.

metaphor   A kind of figurative language that compares one person or object to another, as in the phrase "the arrows of snow."

meter   A recurring, rhythmic beat in a poetic line.

metonymy   A kind of figurative language in which the name of one thing is applied to the whole thing with which it is associated, as in "The stormgray sea yields to his prows."

Naturalism   A nineteenth-century literary movement, especially in France, that stressed the objective role of the novelist. Emile Zola compared the novelist to the experimental scientist and stressed determinism based on heredity and environment.

ode   Originally a Greek form, a lyric poem that praises a person or an object, such as "Ode to Joy."

pathetic fallacy   A literary device in which nature reflects the poet's feelings.

protagonist   The main character of a piece of fiction.

pseudonym   A false literary or pen name.

Realism   A nineteenth-century movement that stressed truthful representation of the world in literature. Details of everyday life were important in Realist works.

Romanticism   An artistic movement that began in Germany at the end of the eighteenth century and spread to the rest of Europe and America in the nineteenth century. The Romantics stressed the artist's sensations and impressions.

scene A brief portion of a play; occurs in a single place.

setting The location of the action of a play or piece of fiction.

Shakespearean sonnet A 14-line poem consisting of three quatrains and a couplet, with a rhyme scheme of *abab cdcd efef gg*.

simile A comparison using *like* or *as*.

sonnet A 14-line lyric poem. The first three stanzas state a problem that is resolved in the final stanza.

tragedy A drama in which the main character suffers a decline or, in modern plays, dies.

Appendix: Genre Descriptions

Drama: Comedy
(Chapter 13)

Drama is the oldest and most popular literary form. Its origins are rooted in ritual dance and song, with certain members of a group acting out roles while others form the audience. The interaction between the actors and the audience is necessary to the play. Generally, if the drama turns out well, it is called a comedy. The main character undergoes some minor difficulties that are resolved during the play. Chekhov's comedies resemble the *comedy of manners,* in which the behavior and relationships of ladies and gentlemen are gently ridiculed.

Drama: Tragedy
(Chapter 4, 8)

Serious drama that ends in death or suffering for the main character (protagonist) is called a tragedy. Tragedy is performed throughout the world, but in the West it has been shaped by the ancient Greeks. In his *Poetics,* Aristotle (383–322 B.C.E.) analyzes the tragedy as "an imitation of an action"—that is, role-playing—to show the decline of a noble character. The suffering of the protagonist and his efforts to avoid his fate bring the audience to a sense of fear and pity. The shared emotional effect of the tragedy and its sad ending brings the audience together as a community.

Shakespeare and other tragedians of the Elizabethan age wrote several types of tragedies, including the *revenge tragedy,* that involved complicated plots, adultery, incest, and multiple murders. Shakespeare's *Romeo and Juliet* is an experimental tragedy that has been criticized for the major role played by chance in the death of the two lovers. However, earlier prose forms—such as the novels of chivalry—had already hinted at the potential tragic consequences of uncontrolled young love.

Fiction: Novel
(Chapter 11, 16, 17, 18, 19, 23, 24, 26)

The art of storytelling can entertain us, let us experience events vicariously, or help us understand ourselves or others. Even though the events of a story may seem real (*Praisesong for the Widow*) or fantastic (the dream in *O Pioneers!*), the author carefully uses language to create a fictional world. The longest fictional form is the novel, which narrates a series of events, called the *plot*, about a number of people, the *characters*. A novel may have several plots or subplots, and many characters. An important quality of fiction is the *tone*, or the way in which the author shows a particular attitude or feeling toward the subject. Tone, especially *irony*, is important in Dickens's fiction. In Dinesen's fiction, a special *atmosphere* and *setting* are also important.

Fiction: Novella
(Chapter 12, 21)

The novella is narrative fiction which is longer than a short story and shorter than a novel. It usually concentrates on fewer matters than a novel and has fewer characters. Most novellas, including *The Turn of the Screw*, have no subplots, but they do possess a complex structure, frequently a framed story or a story within a story. The structure of *Chronicle of a Death Foretold* is very complicated because the author presents the same events several times, but each telling is from the perspective of a different character.

Fiction: Philosophical Novel
(Chapter 20)

A distinctive feature of the modern novel is the use of important intellectual currents as a framework. For example, in the late nineteenth century the world was shaken by the radical view of Karl Marx, put forth in his book *Das Capital* (1867–1884), that history was a struggle between the capitalist middle class and the workers. Marx believed this class conflict would be won by the workers through revolution. Other important intellectual works of the late nineteenth-century were Charles Darwin's *Origin of Species* (1859) and Sigmund Freud's 1899 work *Interpretation of Dreams*. Both helped to undermine the confidence in human beings as rational creatures. Modern Western philosophers such as Nietzsche and Sartre have promoted a view of the universe as indifferent to human suffering. In their view, God does not exist. These intellectual views are reflected in the modern existentialist novel with its underlying sense of disillusion and emptiness.

Fiction: Short Story
(Chapter 5, 6, 14, 15, 22)

In the Western world, the briefest written fictional form is the short story. It has a single plot, few characters, and is told in prose. In Asia, however, the short story combines prose and poetry. The traditional Chinese short story is based on the ancient practice of storytellers entertaining the public at periodic festivals such as the New Year's celebration. Storytellers drew from their oral tradition and frequently included important historical figures and political events in their tales. In both East and West, the short story has a carefully controlled structure, with a beginning, middle, and end. The ending usually brings a climax that shocks or surprises the reader. The master of the short story in the West is the American Edgar Allan Poe (1809–1849).

Nonfiction: Autobiographical Essay
(Chapter 10)

Essay comes from the Old French *essai*, meaning "to try"; it was established by Montaigne in the sixteenth century. It is normally a brief prose composition that makes a point or persuades an audience, usually in an informal manner.

Poetry: Epic or Heroic Poem
(Chapter 1, 3)

Since the time of the ancient Greeks, the epic or heroic poem has formed an important part of the Western literary tradition. The Greeks of the fifth and sixth centuries B.C.E. (Before the Common Era) believed that their culture had in its past a golden age between the Iron and Bronze ages when great heroes fought battles at the cities of Thebes and Troy. Long after that Heroic period, in the eighth century B.C.E., Homer drew on oral tradition to compose his epic poems, The Iliad and The Odyssey. Both his works are traditional epics—that is, they are based on historical figures who represent the ideal of a culture or nation united by language, religion, and customs.

Poetry: Free Verse
(Chapter 25)

Although it is written with the typical short lines of poetry, free verse (unlike most poetry) has no regular meter or beat, and usually no rhyme.

Poetry: Odes and Sonnets
(Chapter 8, 9)

The ode is an ancient poetic form dating back to the Greeks. It is also the most formal and complex lyric form, which is used to praise someone or something in a stately, ceremonial way. The lyric form is closest to poetry's musical origin (the lyre is a musical instrument) and is written in the first person ("I"). A second poetic form, the sonnet, usually expresses personal feelings about love, death, or other emotional issues. The Elizabethan sonnet is a 14-line poem divided into three quatrains (a group of four lines) and a couplet (two lines). Although it may vary, usually the rhyme scheme is *abab cdcd efef gg*.

Poetry: Verse Narrative
(Chapter 7)

Although its main point is to tell a story, verse narrative is written in poetic form. The lines are rhythmic and usually rhyme in pairs (couplets). Chaucer introduced into English the *heroic couplet*, with a meter called *iambic pentameter* (five metrical units or *feet*, each having one unstressed and one stressed syllable).

Prose: Sacred Text
(Chapter 2, 25)

The best-known sacred texts are associated with world religions: the Jewish Torah, the Christian New Testament, the Moslem Koran. Others have only recently been recorded from oral tradition. Each sacred text is an ancient source of wisdom that teaches a world view and a code of moral behavior.

Acknowledgments *(continued from copyright page)*

Marie de France. Excerpt from Chapter IV, "Bisclavret" pp. 68–72 *The Lais of Marie de France* translated by Glyn S. Burgress and Keith Busby (Penguin Classics, 1986), Translation copyright © Glyn S. Burgress and Keith Busby, 1986. Reproduced by permission of Penguin Books Ltd., London, England.

Chaucer, Geoffrey. 257 lines from "The Miller's Tale" (pp 105-122) from *The Canterbury Tales* by Geoffrey Chaucer, translated by Nevill Coghill (Penguin Classics, Revised edition 1977), copyright © 1951 by Nevill Coghill, 1958, 1960, 1975, 1977.

Shakespeare, William. Excerpt from *The Tragedy of Romeo and Juliet.* Evans, G. Blakemore (Editor), *The Riverside Shakespeare.* Copyright © 1974 by Houghton Mifflin Company. Used with permission.

Wharton, Edith. Excerpt from "Roman Fever." Adapted with the permission of Charles Scribner's Sons, an imprint of MacMillan Publishing Company from *Roman Fever and Other Stories* by Edith Wharton. Copyright 1934 by Liberty Magazine, renewed © 1962 by William R. Tyler.

Kafka, Franz. Excerpt from "The Metamorphosis." From *The Metamorphosis* by Franz Kafka, trans. by Willa and Edwin Muir. Copyright 1946, 1948 by Schocken Books Inc. Reprinted by permission of Schocken Books, published by Pantheon Books, a division of Random House, Inc. Reprinted by permission of Martin Secker and Warburg Limited.

Cather, Willa. Excerpt from *O Pioneers.* Reprinted by permission of Virago Press.

She, Lao. Excerpt from "Rickshaw." From *Rickshaw* (the novel *Lo-T'o Hsiang Tsu*) by Lao She translated by Jean M. James. Reprinted by permission of the University of Hawaii Press. Copyright © 1979 by the Univeristy of Hawaii Press. Published originally in the serial form in the periodical *Yu-chou-feng* September 1936 to May 1937.

Achebe, Chinua. Excerpt from *Things Fall Apart.* Reprinted by permission of William Heinemann Limited.

Dinesen, Isak. Excerpt from *Out of Africa.* From *Out of Africa* by Isak Dinesen. Copyright 1937 by Random House, Inc. and renewed 1965 by Rungstediundfonden. Reprinted by permission of Random House, Inc. Copyright 1937, 1938 by Random House, Inc. Copyright renewed by Rungstedlung Foundation.

Abe, Kobo. Excerpt from *Woman in the Dunes.* From *The Woman in the Dunes* by Kobo Abe, trans., E. Dale Saunders. Copyright © 1964 Alfred A. Knopf, Inc. Reprinted by permission of Alfred A. Knopf, Inc. and Martin Secker and Warburg Limited.

García Márquez, Gabriel. Excerpt from *Chronicle of a Death Foretold.* From *Chronicle of a Death Foretold* by Gabriel García Márquez, trans., G. Rabassa. Translation copyright © 1982 by Alfred A. Knopf, Inc. Reprinted by permission of Alfred A. Knopf, Inc. and Random Century Group. Published in the British Commonwealth by Jonathan Cape.

Munro, Alice. Excerpt from "Boys and Girls." Reprinted from Alice Munro, "Boys and Girls" in *Dance of the Happy Shades,* 1968. Reprinted by permission of McGraw-Hill Ryerson Limited. Excerpted from "Boys and Girls," story included in the collection *Dance of the Happy Shades* by Alice Munro, copyright © 1968 by Alice Munro. Reprinted by permission of the Virginia Barber Literary Agency, Inc.

Desai, Anita. Excerpt from *Fire on the Mountain* by Anita Desai. Copyright © 1977 by Anita Desai. Reprinted by permission of Harper Collins Publishers Inc. and Rogers, Coleridge & White Ltd.

Mahfouz, Naguib. Excerpt from *The Thief and the Dogs.* From *The Thief and the Dogs* by Naguib Mahfouz, translated by Trevor Le Gassich. Translation copyright © 1984 by The American University in Cairo Press. Used by permission of Doubleday, a division of Bantam Doubleday Dell Publishing Group, Inc.

Alegría, Claribel. "Flowers from the Volcano." Reprinted from *Flowers from the Volcano,* by Claribel Alegría, translated by Carolyn Forché, by permission of the University of Pittsburgh Press. © 1982 by Claribel Alegría and Carolyn Forché

Leon-Portilla, Miguel. Excerpt from *Pre-Columbian Literature of Mexico.* From *Pre-Columbian Literature of Mexico* by Miguel Leon-Portilla. Copyright 1969 by the University of Oklahoma Press.

Marshall, Paule. Excerpt from *Praisesong for the Widow.* Reprinted by permission of The Putnam Publishing Group from *Praisesong for the Widow* by Paule Marshall. Copyright © 1983 by Paule Marshall. This excerpt was reprinted with the permission of Paule Marshall.

Index

Abe, Kobo, 155
Achebe, Chinua, 143
Africa, 143
"Ain't I a Woman?", 87
Alegría, Claribel, 191
Antigone, 29
autobiographical essay, 87, 213

"Bisclavret", 49
"Boys and Girls", 169
Buddhism, 39, 176

Canada, 169
Canterbury Tales, The, 57
Caribbean, 201
Cather, Willa, 131
Central America, 191
Chaucer, Geoffrey, 57, 214
Chekhov, Anton, 109, 211
China, 39, 137
Chronicle of a Death Foretold, 161, 212
Colombia, 162
Confucianism, 39
courtly love, 49, 57
cuneiform, 3

Darwin, Charles, 183, 212
Denmark, 149
Desai, Anita, 175
Dickens, Charles, 93, 137, 183, 212
Dinesen, Isak, 149, 212
drama
    comedy, 109, 209, 211
    tragedy, 29, 69, 210, 211

Egypt, 183
Elizabethan sonnet, 214
England, 57, 69, 81, 93
epic, 23, 213
essay, 213
Existentialism, 155, 156, 184, 212

feminist, 176
fiction
    novel, 93, 131, 137, 143, 149, 175, 183, 201, 211–12

novella, 99, 161, 212
philosphical novel, 155, 212
short story, 39, 49, 117, 125, 169, 212–13
Fire on the Mountain, 175
"Flowers from the Volcano", 191
France, Marie de, 49
Freud, Sigmund, 100, 126, 183, 212

García Márquez, Gabriel, 161
Genesis, 13
Germany, 79
Gothic, 99, 155, 209
Greece, 23, 29

Hebrew, 13
Hinduism, 175, 176
Homer, 23
"Huluppu-Tree, The", 3
Inanna, Queen of Heaven and Earth, 3
India, 175

James, Henry, 99, 117
Japan, 155

Kafka, Franz, 125, 155
Lais of Marie de France, The, 49
Lao She, 137

Magical Realism, 161, 209
Mahfouz, Naguib, 183
Manchuria, 155
Marshall, Paule, 201
Marxism, 183, 191, 192, 212
Mesopotamia, 3
"Metamorphosis, The", 125
"Miller's Tale, The", 57
Munro, Alice, 169
"My Heart Leaps Up When I Behold", 83

Nicaragua, 191
Nietzsche, Friedrich, 212
Nigeria, 143
nonfiction
    autobiographical essay, 87, 213
    novel, 211

O Pioneers!, 131, 212
ode, 33, 209
"Ode to Joy", 80
"Ode to Man", 33
Odyssey, The, 23
Oliver Twist, 93
oral tradition, 3, 13, 20, 183, 197,
    201, 213, 214
  sacred text, 13, 20, 214
Out of Africa, 149

poem, 3, 213
poetry, 13, 213
  epic, 3, 23, 213
  free verse, 191, 213
  heroic poem, 3, 23, 213
  lyric, 213–14
  ode, 79, 213–14
  sacred text, 197, 214
  sonnet, 78, 79, 210, 213–14
  verse narrative, 57, 214
Praisesong for the Widow, 201, 212

Realism, 137, 170, 183, 209
"Red Thread Maiden", 39
Rickshaw, 137
"Roman Fever", 117
Romantic, 79, 81, 100, 131
Romanticism, 79, 183, 209–10

Romeo and Juliet, 69, 211
Russia, 109

Sacred Hymn of Sacrifice to
    Tlaloc, 197
Sartre, Jean Paul, 212
Schiller, Johann Friedrich von, 79, 80
Shakespeare, William, 69, 210, 211
"Sonnet 29", 78, 210, 214
Sophocles, 29
Sumer, 3

"The World Is Too Much with Us; Late
    and Soon", 83
Thief and the Dogs, The, 183
Things Fall Apart, 143
"To Toussaint L'Ouverture", 82
Truth, Sojourner, 87
Turn of the Screw, The, 99, 212

Uncle Vanya, 109
United States, 20, 87, 99, 117

Wharton, Edith, 117
Woman in the Dunes, The, 155
Wordsworth, William, 81

Yuan Chiao, 39

About the Authors

Carole M. Shaffer-Koros is professor and chair of the Department of English/ESL at Kean College of New Jersey and a former director of the ESL program there. She has taught a broad range of literature and language courses as well as developmental English, ESL, and Spanish. She was recently elected vice-president of the International Edith Wharton Society.

Jessie M. Reppy is an associate professor of ESL at Kean College of New Jersey and is a former director of the ESL program there. She has been an ESL teacher and administrator—both in the U.S. and overseas—for 25 years. Throughout her career she has been active in state and national professional associations, including TESOL, New Jersey State TESOL-BE, and New York State TESOL, and has served on the boards of the two state affiliates.

Explorations in World Literature grew out of a New Jersey Humanities grant awarded to both instructors in 1988.

DATE	AFRICA	AMERICAS
3200 B.C.E.		
2000 B.C.E.		
1000 B.C.E.		
900 B.C.E.		
700 B.C.E.		
500 B.C.E.		
400 B.C.E.		
100 B.C.E.		
0		
800 C.E.		
1000		
1100		
1200		
1300		
1400		
1500		
1600		
1700		
1800		
1900		